はしがき

　東京オリンピックが 2020 年 7 月 24 日から 8 月 9 日までの 17 日間、パラリンピックが同年 8 月 25 日から 9 月 6 日までの 13 日間、開催されます。それに伴い世界各国から多くの人が日本を訪れることになるので、多言語や多文化への対応がとても大事になります。中でも英語がコミュニケーションのツールとして大切な〔　　　〕言うまでもありません。日本を訪れた人々が日本を好きに〔　　　　　　　　〕、「おもてなし」を充実させたいものです。

　このテキストは、語学学習における 4 技能の中〔　　　　　　　　　〕ングのスキルを向上させ、音声を中心にコミュニケーション〔　　　　　　〕ることを目的としています。作成に当たっては、著者のアメリカ、イギリス、オーストラリア等での生活体験、民間企業の海外営業部での勤務経験などから得たことをできるだけ多く取り入れ、英語ネイティブが日常的に使うオーセンティックな英語表現を修得できるように心がけました。主人公アオイは神戸の大学を卒業後イギリスに本社のある大手商社の大阪支社に就職し、転勤でシンガポールに赴任します。国内外のビジネスシーンと関連させた場面を設定しているため、英語学習のみならず学習者のビジネスに対する知的好奇心も刺激することになると確信しています。各ユニットは 4 ページで構成され、全部で 15 のユニットから成ります。

Words & Phrases

各ユニットに出てくる重要な単語やフレーズの適切な意味を、与えられたものの中から選び、学びます。

Warm-up

状況設定に応じた短いダイアログの空所を与えられた選択肢の中から選び補充した後、音声を聴いて質問に英語で答える問題があります。

Exercise 1

並べかえ英作文を完成した後、音声を聴いてその英文を確認する問題があります。

Exercise 2

音声を聴いて空所を補充した後、与えられた日本語の文の中から適切な意味を選ぶ問題があります。

Exercise 3

音声を聴いて空所を補充する問題と、質問に対する答を与えられた選択肢の中から選ぶ問題があります。

Challenge Corner 1

音声を聴いて、質問に対する答を与えられた選択肢の中から選ぶ問題があります。

Challenge Corner 2

音声を聴いて書き取る問題と、質問に対する答を与えられた選択肢の中から選ぶ問題があります。

本テキストに準備されている音声を聴きながら、英語ネイティブがビジネスシーンや日常的に使っている表現を繰り返し何度もリスニングをしたり、シャドーイングをしたり、スピーキングの練習をしたりすれば、リスニングスキルはもちろんのこと、スピーキング、リーディング、ライティングのスキルも知らず知らずのうちに確実に向上していくでしょう。特にリスニングスキルをアップさせたい学習者にとって、本テキストは必ず役に立つはずです。また、同時に、ビジネスシーンで使われる英語表現を覚えることができます。学習者の皆さんの弛み無い努力を期待しています。

　このテキストは学習者の英語習熟度に応じて、半期でも通年でも使用することができます。半期で使用する場合は1ユニットを1回の授業で、通年で使用する場合は小テストや復習テストなどを行いながら、半期でユニット8まで終わることを目安としてください。

　最後に、テキスト作成にあたり様々なアドバイスをしてくださった松柏社の森有紀子氏に心から御礼申し上げます。

　　　2019年10月

行時　潔
今川　京子
Antony J. Parker

Contents

1	A Job at Last		採用面接試験	06
2	Singapore Transfer		海外転勤の内示 1	10
3	On the Plane		飛行機内では	14
4	At Changi Airport: Lion City, Here I Am!		シンガポール支社へ	18
5	First Posting		アパートを決める	22
6	What a Cozy Place!		引っ越し作業	26
7	First Day on the Job in Singapore		シンガポール支社勤務初日	30
8	Meeting a Business Client		商談に行く	34
9	Making New Friends		友だちができる	38
10	Wining and Dining		接待のための準備	42
11	Health Problems and Other Issues		体調をくずしたら	46
12	A Sales Presentation & Customer Complaints		プレゼン／クレーム処理	50
13	Catching up with an Old Friend in Perth		有給休暇をとってパースへ	54
14	A Business Trip to Indonesia and Hong Kong		出張―インドネシア／香港	58
15	A New Assignment		海外転勤の内示 2	62

Characters

Aoi

外資系商社（本部はロンドン）の大阪支社に4月に入社して海外事業部所属。9月初旬にシンガポール支社への転勤の内示をもらう。入社半年後（10月）にシンガポール支社に赴任。シンガポールでは事業部に所属。

Maya Chung

シンガポール支社勤務で入社5年目。事業部に所属。7月に出張で大阪支社にやって来る。

Michael Fong

シンガポール支社の事業部課長。ジェフ・フーとは高校時代からの友人。

Jeffrey Peterson

シンガポール支社長で、アオイが赴任した10月はシドニーに出張中。

Steve Gordon

大阪支社長で11月にホノルル支社へ転勤予定。

▶ A Business Client ◀

Jeff Foo

シンガポールの取引先（スパイスの会社）の営業部門の担当者。

▶ Friends ◀

Chris & Dolly White

サンフランシスコ出身でIT関係の仕事でシンガポールに10月から来年の3月まで滞在予定。

Emily's Family

夫婦

Emily エミリー
アオイの友人でパース在住。

Joan ジョーン
アトキンス夫人。
エミリーの母。

Bob ボブ
アトキンス氏。
エミリーの父。

Perth

親子

Judy & Peggy Watanabe
ジュディとペギー

サンフランシスコ在住で
アオイとアオイの母の友人。

San Francisco

Unit 1

A Job at Last

採用面接試験

大学4年生のアオイは外資系商社への就職活動中。学生時代に短期留学で訪れたサンフランシスコやロサンゼルス、そしてオーストラリアからの留学生エミリーと一緒に行ったオーストラリアかシンガポールで活躍したいと思っている。悪戦苦闘の末ようやく念願の外資系商社への就職が決まる。

次の1～8の語または語句の最も適切な意味を下のa～hから選びましょう。
次に音声を聴いて単語の発音を確認しましょう。

● Audio 1-02

1. apply to	**2.** trading company	**3.** mock	**4.** confidence
5. conviction	**6.** wander	**7.** relocate	**8.** at long last

a. 模擬の　　　　b.（目・視線などが）きょろきょろ見回す　　c. 商社　　d. 転勤する
e. …に応募する　f. やっと（のことで）　　　　g. 強い信念　h. 自信

次の1～3のダイアログの空所に入る最も適切なものをa～cの中から選びましょう。
次に質問の音声を聴いて、各ダイアログについての質問に答えましょう。

On the phone

● Audio 1-03

1. **Emily:** How's your job hunting been going?

　　Aoi: Well, it's been pretty tough. [1]_____ seventeen trading companies already.

　　Emily: Wow! That many? Why do you want to work for a trading company?

　　Answer

2. **Aoi:** [2]_____ mock interviews.

　　Emily: So you must be ready for the real thing by now.

　　Aoi: Yes. But I don't have any confidence. Can you give me some advice?

　　Answer

3. **Emily:** When interviewed, speak with passion and conviction.

　　Aoi: All right. [3]_____ that.

　　Emily: And don't let your eyes wander. Eye contact with the interviewer is very important.

　　Answer

a. I've been taking　　b. I think I can do　　c. I've applied to

1〜7の（　　）内の語または語句を並べかえて英文を完成させましょう。ただし、文頭にくるものも小文字で与えています。次に音声を聴いて答を確認しましょう。

● Audio 1-04

1. 10 時からの面接でこちらに来ました。
(a, for, I'm, ten, here, interview, o'clock).

_____

2. 私はマイペースで物事をしてしまいがちです。
(tend, do, I, at, things, own pace, to, my).

_____

3. 業績はどのように評価されますか？
(be, will, my, how, evaluated, performance)?

_____

4. 弊社についてどのようなことを知っていますか？
(know, company, you, what, this, do, about)?

_____

5. あなたは管理者に対して何を望みますか？
(expect, do, supervisor, from, what, you, a)?

_____

6. あなたの最大の長所と短所は何ですか？
(are, greatest, your, and weaknesses, what, strengths)?

_____

7. 5 年後、あなたはどうなっていたいですか？
(see, in, you, where, yourself, do, five years)?

_____

Exercise 2　音声を聴いて、1〜5 の空所を埋めましょう。次に a 〜 e の日本語の文の中から適切な意味をそれぞれ選び、英文の右の空欄に記入しましょう。

● Audio 1-05

1. What [1] _____ [2] _____ does your company offer?　_____

2. How do you [3] _____ [4] _____?　_____

3. What do you do in your [5] _____ [6] _____?　_____

4. What can you [7] _____ [8] _____ this company?　_____

5. What was the most [9] _____ [10] _____ at university?　_____

a. プレッシャーにどのように対応していますか？　　b. 福利厚生はどうなってますでしょうか？
c. 大学で最もやりがいのあった講義はどんなものでしたか？　　d. 弊社にどのような貢献ができますか？
e. 余暇は何をしていますか？

Exercise 3　音声を聴いて、ダイアログの空所 1 ～ 4 を埋めましょう。次に 1 と 2 の質問に対して最も適切な答を a ～ c の中から選びましょう。

At the job interview　　　　　　　　　　　● Audio 1-06

Mr. Simon:　Hello, Ms. Manabe. I'm Phil Simon. It's nice to meet you.

こんにちは、マナベさん。私はフィル・サイモンです。初めまして。

Aoi:　Hello, Mr. Simon. It's (　　　　) (　　　　).

こんにちは。お会いできて光栄です、サイモンさん。

Mr. Simon:　How did you get here today?

今日はどうやって来られましたか？

Aoi:　I (　　　　) (　　　　) (　　　　).

電車で来ました。

Mr. Simon:　Did you have any trouble finding us?

弊社は探しにくかったですか？

Aoi:　No, not at all. It was easy getting here.

いいえ。簡単にわかりました。とてもわかりやすい場所でした。

Mr. Simon:　OK. Now, can you tell me a bit about yourself?

それは良かった。さて、あなたについて少し教えていただけますか？

Aoi:　Sure. I'm a university student in Kobe…and I like trying new things.

(　　　　) (　　　　).

はい。神戸にある大学の学生です。……私は新しいことにチャレンジすることが好きです。

以上です。

Mr. Simon:　So, why are you interested in working for us?

弊社で働きたいと思った理由を教えてくれますか？

Aoi:　Well, there are (　　　　) (　　　　) (　　　　) I'd like to work for this company…

御社で働きたい理由は 3 つありまして……

1. Was it difficult for Aoi to find the interview venue?
　　a. Yes, it was.　　　b. No, it wasn't.　　　c. We don't know.

2. Where does Aoi go to university?
　　a. In Kobe　　　b. In Osaka　　　c. In Tokyo

Challenge Corner

Audio 1-07

残りのダイアログを聴いて、1～3の質問に対して最も適切な答をa～cの中から選びましょう。

Osaka city

1. Which foreign branch did Aoi mention?
   a. Honolulu   b. Sydney   c. San Francisco

2. How many foreign places did Mr. Simon mention?
   a. Three   b. Four   c. Five

3. Does Aoi mind working at one of the foreign branches?
   a. Yes, she does.   b. No, she doesn't.   c. We can't tell.

Challenge Corner

ダイアログの音声を聴いて、＿＿の部分を書き取り、1と2の質問に対して最も適切な答をa～cの中から選びましょう。

On the phone

Audio 1-08

Aoi: Guess what? I have some good news to tell you!

Emily: Don't tell me that you'll be coming to Perth to visit me.

Aoi: No, not yet. At long last, ＿＿＿＿＿＿＿＿ .

1. What is Aoi's good news about?
   a. Her visit to Perth   b. Her new job   c. Neither a nor b

▶▶▶▶ ◀◀◀◀   Audio 1-09

Emily: So, where do you start working?

Aoi: I don't know yet. ＿＿＿＿＿＿＿＿ .

Emily: But, you applied to work in Sydney or Singapore, right?

2. Which branch is Aoi most likely to work at?
   a. The Sydney branch
   b. The Singapore branch
   c. The Osaka branch

採用面接試験

Unit 2

Singapore Transfer

海外転勤の内示 1

アオイが就職して早3カ月、ようやく仕事にも慣れてきた。そんな中、シンガポール支社から出張でやって来たマヤ・チュングを関西国際空港まで迎えに行き、休日には大阪、京都、そして神戸を案内。9月初旬、アオイは支社長のスティーブ・ゴードンから10月からのシンガポール赴任の内示を受ける。

 次の1〜8の語または語句の最も適切な意味を下のa〜hから選びましょう。
次に音声を聴いて単語の発音を確認しましょう。

● Audio 1-10

1. fond   **2.** favor   **3.** pick up   **4.** the following

5. take a look at   **6.** tourist   **7.** transfer   **8.** let down

a. 旅行者	b. (人)をがっかりさせる	c. 楽しい	d. (人)を車で迎えに行く
e. …へ転任させる	f. …をちょっと見る	g. 次の	h. お願い

 次の1〜3のダイアログの空所に入る最も適切なものをa〜cの中から選びましょう。
次に質問の音声を聴いて、各ダイアログについての質問に答えましょう。

At the office   ● Audio 1-11

1. Mr. Gordon: We're having Maya Chung from the Singapore branch visit us next week.

    Aoi: From Singapore? I do ¹ _____ of Singapore.

    Mr. Gordon: I didn't know you'd been there.

    Answer

2. Mr. Gordon: Aoi, would you do me a favor?

    Aoi: Sure, Mr. Gordon. What can I do for you?

    Mr. Gordon: Will you ² _____ from Kanku?

    Answer

3. Aoi: How long will she be with us?

    Mr. Gordon: She'll be here from next Wednesday till Tuesday of the following week.

    Aoi: Okay. I'll ³ _____ Osaka, Kyoto, and Kobe.

    Answer

    a. show her around   b. pick up Maya   c. have fond memories

Exercise 1　1〜7の（　）内の語または語句を並べかえて英文を完成させましょう。ただし、文頭にくるものも小文字で与えています。次に音声を聴いて答を確認しましょう。

● Audio 1-12

1. 大阪支社にようこそ。

(you, I'd, branch, to, the, welcome, like, Osaka, to).

_____

2. 川崎君を紹介します。

(to, let, you, Mr. Kawasaki, introduce, me).

_____

3. 良き上司に恵まれて最高です。

(such, lucky, boss, a, have, to, I'm, good).

_____

4. 私は競い合える同僚と働くことが大好きです。

(working, competitive, I, workers, love, with, fellow).

_____

5. 職場には尊敬できる先輩がたくさんいます。

(senior, there, workers, are, respect, many, I) at work.

_____

6. 彼は外資系の商社に勤めています。

(for, trading, he, foreign, a, works, company).

_____

7. 海外赴任の夢がかないました。

(abroad, dream, true, my, work, has, to, come).

_____

Exercise 2　音声を聴いて、1〜5の空所を埋めましょう。次にa〜eの日本語の文の中から適切な意味をそれぞれ選び、英文の右の空欄に記入しましょう。

● Audio 1-13

1. Have you [1] _____ [2] _____ [3] _____ the new job yet?　_____

2. How many [4] _____ [5] _____ [6] _____ at the same time?　_____

3. Do you have a [7] _____ [8] _____?　_____

4. How long will you be working for a [9] _____ [10] _____?　_____

5. Was your [11] _____ [12] _____ to Tokyo for two nights?　_____

a. 海外の子会社にはどれくらい駐在するのですか？　b. 同期入社はどれくらいいますか？

c. 新しい仕事にはもう慣れましたか？　　　　　　d. 東京出張は2泊3日でしたか？

e. お名刺をいただけますか？

Exercise 　音声を聴いて、ダイアログの空所 1 ～ 4 を埋めましょう。次に 1 と 2 の質問に対して最も
適切な答を a ～ c の中から選びましょう。

🔊 **Audio 1-14**

Kansai Airport Station

© Aisyaqilumaranas / Shutterstock.com

At Kansai International Airport

Aoi: So, how was ( ) ( ), Maya?
ところで、飛行機の旅はいかがでしたか、マヤ？

Maya: It wasn't too smooth because of turbulence. That's why we got here thirty minutes late.
乱気流のため良くなかったです。だから、30 分遅れて到着しました。

Aoi: Geez. I'm sorry to hear that. Are you all right?
あらまあ。それはお気の毒に。大丈夫ですか？

Maya: Yeah, I'm OK. ( ) ( ) ( ).
ええ、大丈夫です。お気遣いありがとう。

Aoi: I hope your job goes well and you enjoy your time here in Japan.
ここ日本でのお仕事が上手く行き滞在をお楽しみいただけるよう願っています。

Maya: Thank you. By the way, have you ever heard of the Japanese comic, *Naruto*?
ありがとう。ところで、日本の漫画、『ナルト』は聞いたことありますか？

Aoi: Sure. I really enjoyed it. Have you ever ( ) ( )?
はい。とても楽しんでそれを読みました。読んだことありますか？

Maya: Of course. Ever since I read it, I've been attracted to Japanese subculture.
もちろん。それを読んでから、私は日本のサブカルチャーに魅了されてきました。

Aoi: Sounds like you and I will ( ) ( ) ( ).
私たち気が合うようですね。

Maya: Sounds like it! I'm super thrilled now.
そのようね！今とてもワクワクしています。

1. How long was Maya's flight delayed?
   a. Fifteen minutes　　b. Thirty minutes　　c. Forty-five minutes

2. Who has read *Naruto*?
   a. Aoi　　　　　b. Maya　　　　　c. Both Aoi and Maya

Challenge Corner 1

Audio 1-15

残りのダイアログを聴いて、1～3の質問に対して最も適切な答をa～cの中から選びましょう。

Yasaka-shrine　　　Kazamidori no Yakata　　　A bus stop in Kitano district　　　Kyoto station

1. Where will Aoi and Maya visit this weekend?
　　a. Kyoto　　　　　　　b. Kobe　　　　　　　c. Both Kyoto and Kobe

2. When will they go to Kobe?
　　a. On Saturday　　　　b. On Sunday　　　　c. It is not mentioned.

3. Has Maya read the tourist guidebooks yet?
　　a. Yes, she has.　　　b. No, she hasn't.　　　c. We can't tell.

Challenge Corner 2

ダイアログの音声を聴いて、　　の部分を書き取り、1と2の質問に対して最も適切な答をa～cの中から選びましょう。

Audio 1-16

▶▶▶▶　◀◀◀◀

Mr. Gordon: Aoi, the company will soon be announcing that

Aoi: Me? Really? To which branch?

Mr. Gordon: To the Singapore branch. I'm sure you'll do a great job there.

Aoi: Thank you so much, Mr. Gordon. I won't let you down.

1. When will Aoi be transferred to the Singapore branch?
　　a. In September　　　b. In October　　　c. In November

Audio 1-17

▶▶▶▶　◀◀◀◀

Mr. Gordon: Have you let Maya know about your transfer to Singapore?

Aoi: 　　　　　　　　　till it was announced by the company.

Mr. Gordon: Good. It'll be announced tomorrow, so you can tell her then.

Aoi: Wow! Tomorrow is going to be a big day for me.

2. Has Aoi already informed Maya of her transfer to Singapore?
　　a. Yes, she has.　　　b. No, she hasn't.　　　c. We don't know.

Unit 3

On the Plane

飛行機内では

アオイはシンガポール支社に1年間赴任することに。シンガポールには学生時代オーストラリアのパース出身のエミリーと一緒に訪れた。ちょっと暑いが住み心地が良さそうで、ここで仕事をしてみたいと思っていた。大阪支社の仲間に見送られ、関西国際空港からシンガポールに向けていざ出発！

次の1～8の語または語句の最も適切な意味を下のa～hから選びましょう。
次に音声を聴いて単語の発音を確認しましょう。

● Audio 1-18

1. aisle　　**2.** luggage　　**3.** overhead　　**4.** another

5. on vacation　　**6.** sort　　**7.** trade in　　**8.** colleague

a. 手荷物	b. 同僚	c. 通路	d. 休暇で
e. 別の	f. 種類	g. 頭上の	h. …を扱う

次の1～3のダイアログの空所に入る最も適切なものをa～cの中から選びましょう。
次に質問の音声を聴いて、各ダイアログについての質問に答えましょう。

On the plane

● Audio 1-19

➤FA=Flight Attendant

1. Aoi: Where is seat 34H, please?

FA: 34H… let me see. ¹_____ this aisle and it's on your left.

Aoi: Thank you.

Answer

2. FA: Is this your luggage?

Aoi: Yes, it is.

FA: ²_____ you put it in the overhead locker.

Answer

3. Aoi: This headset seems to be broken. Can you get me another one?

FA: Sure. ³_____ a minute? I'll be right back with another one.

Aoi: OK. Thank you.

Answer

　a. Go down　　b. Could you give　　c. Let me help

● 〰️ Audio 1-20

1. 日本語を話せる乗務員はいますか？

(a, attendant, who, there, Japanese, flight, is, speaks)?

_____

2. アルコール飲料は有料ですか？

(drinks, you, for, charge, do, alcoholic)?

_____

3. 何か暖かい飲み物はありますか？

(hot, have, to, do, drink, anything, you)?

_____

4. あの席に移動してもいいですか？

(seat, to, may, that, move, I)?

_____

5. お席をお立ちいただいて結構です。

(about, free, the cabin, move, are, to, you).

_____

6. シートベルトをお締めいただけますでしょうか？

(please, seat belt, you, your, fasten, would)?

_____

7. 当機は 30 分ほどで着陸します。

This airplane (be, half an hour, in, will, about, landing).

_____

Exercise 2 音声を聴いて、1〜5の空所を埋めましょう。次に a 〜 e の日本語の文の中から適切な意
味をそれぞれ選び、英文の右の空欄に記入しましょう。   ● 〰️ Audio 1-21

1. Will you return ¹_____ ²_____ to its upright position? _____

2. Would you like an ³_____ ⁴_____, or a window seat? _____

3. Would you please ⁵_____ ⁶_____ the blind? _____

4. What is the ⁷_____ ⁸_____ in Singapore now? _____

5. Do you have anything ⁹_____ ¹⁰_____? _____

a. 現在のシンガポールの天気はどうですか？   b. 何か読む物はありますか？

c. お席は通路側、窓側どちらがよろしいでしょうか？   d. お席をもとの位置にお戻しくださいますか？

e. ブラインドを閉めていただいてもよろしいでしょうか？

Exercise   音声を聴いて、ダイアログの空所 1 〜 4 を埋めましょう。次に 1 と 2 の質問に対して最も
適切な答を a 〜 c の中から選びましょう。

Just before mealtime   • Audio 1-22

FA: Would you like something to drink?

お飲み物はいかがですか？

Aoi: Could I have some water and (   ) (   ) (   ) coffee?

お水とコーヒーをください。

FA: Of course. Do you take cream and sugar in your coffee?

かしこまりました。お砂糖とミルクはどうなさいますか？

Aoi: No sugar. Just cream, please.

お砂糖は要りません。ミルクだけお願いします。

FA: Sure. (   ) (   ) (   ), sir?

かしこまりました。そちらのお客様は？

Man: Do you have any wine?

ワインはありますか？

FA: Sure. We have red wine and white wine.

はい。赤ワインと白ワインをご用意できます。

Man: Good. Can I have (   ) (   ) (   ) white wine, please?

じゃあ、白ワインをください。

FA: Certainly... (   ) (   ) (   ).

かしこまりました……どうぞ。

1. How would Aoi like her coffee?
   a. With cream   b. With sugar   c. With cream and sugar

2. What does the man have?
   a. Red wine   b. White wine   c. Both red wine and white wine

16

Challenge Corner 1

Audio 1-23

残りのダイアログを聴いて、1 ～ 3 の質問に対して最も適切な答を a ～ c の中から選びましょう。

1. Where is the man going?
   a. To Singapore　　　　b. To Perth　　　　c. To both Singapore and Perth
2. How many times has Aoi been to Perth?
   a. Never　　　　b. Once　　　　c. It's not mentioned.
3. Who is on vacation?
   a. Aoi　　　　b. The man　　　　c. Both Aoi and the man

Challenge Corner 2

ダイアログの音声を聴いて、　の部分を書き取り、1 と 2 の質問に対して最も適切な答を a ～ c の中から選びましょう。

▶▶▶▶ ◀◀◀◀

Audio 1-24

Aoi: What sort of work do you do?

Man:　　　　　　　　　　　　　　　.

Aoi: So do I. What does your company trade in?

1. Who works for a trading company?
   a. Aoi　　　　b. The man　　　　c. Both Aoi and the man

▶▶▶▶ ◀◀◀◀

Audio 1-25

Man: Is anybody coming to the airport to meet you?

Aoi: Yes.　　　　　　　　　　　is coming to pick me up.

Man: Well, good luck in your new job!

2. Who is picking up Aoi at the airport?
   a. Her friend　　　　b. Her colleague　　　　c. Her classmate

飛行機内では

Unit 4

At Changi Airport: Lion City, Here I Am!

シンガポール支社へ

アオイはシンガポールに到着。3か月前に大阪支社に来たマヤ・チュングに空港でピックアップしてもらい、シンガポール支社に直行。支社長のジェフリー・ピーターソンはオーストラリアに出張中だったので事業部課長のマイケル・フォングにご挨拶。今夜は歓迎会。明日はマヤと一緒にアパート探し。

次の1～8の語または語句の最も適切な意味を下のa～hから選びましょう。
次に音声を聴いて単語の発音を確認しましょう。

● Audio 1-26

1. client　　　**2.** drop by　　　**3.** branch manager　　　**4.** on business

5. on foot　　　**6.** nearby　　　**7.** overseas　　　**8.** over

a. 海外の	b. 徒歩で	c. 顧客・取引先	d. …しながら
e. 支店長	f. …に立ち寄る	g. 近くの	h. 商用で

次の1～3のダイアログの空所に入る最も適切なものをa～cの中から選びましょう。
次に質問の音声を聴いて、各ダイアログについての質問に答えましょう。

In the arrivals lounge

● Audio 1-27

1. Maya: Over here, Aoi. Welcome to Singapore.

　Aoi:　Oh, hi Maya. ¹_____ about three months since I last saw you in Osaka.

　Maya: Right. It's so nice to see you again.

　Answer

2. Aoi:　Thank you very much for coming here to meet me.

　Maya: No problem. ²_____ for about a year, right?

　Aoi:　That's right. I have a lot to learn from you about Singapore and our clients.

　Answer

3. Maya: We'll be dropping by our office in Marina Bay first.

　Aoi:　Sure. Is Mr. Peterson, the branch manager, there today?

　Maya: No. ³_____ to Australia on business.

　Answer

　　a. You'll be here　　　b. He's gone　　　c. It's been

Exercise 1　1～7の（　）内の語または語句を並べかえて英文を完成させましょう。ただし、文頭にくるものも小文字で与えています。次に音声を聴いて答を確認しましょう。

🔊 **Audio 1-28**

1. シンガポールにはどれくらい滞在しますか？

(staying, long, you, will, how, be) in Singapore?

_____

2. 申請する物は何かありますか？

(you, anything, to, have, do, declare)?

_____

3. ここには出張で来ました。

(on, here, trip, I'm, business, a).

_____

4. 遺失物取扱所はどこですか？

(found, is, the, where, lost, and, office)?

_____

5. どこで損害の補償を請求できますか？

(a, can, the damage, I, make, where, for, claim)?

_____

6. ここから都心部まで行くのに最適な方法は何ですか？

(the best way, to, to, what, the city center, is, get) from here?

_____

7. マリーナ地区までのタクシー料金はいくらですか？

(is, the Marina Bay area, how much, taxi fare, to, the)?

_____

Exercise 2　音声を聴いて、1～5の空所を埋めましょう。次に a ～ e の日本語の文の中から適切な意味をそれぞれ選び、英文の右の空欄に記入しましょう。

🔊 **Audio 1-29**

1. ¹_____ ²_____ ³_____ of your visit to Singapore?　　_____

2. ⁴_____ ⁵_____ ⁶_____ Star Travel?　　_____

3. How can I get to the ⁷_____ ⁸_____?　　_____

4. Where is the ⁹_____ ¹⁰_____?　　_____

5. Could you please speak in ¹¹_____ ¹²_____?　　_____

a. 乗り継ぎカウンターはどこですか？　　b. 易しい英語で話してくれますか？

c. スタートラベルの方ですか？　　d. シンガポール訪問の目的は何ですか？

e. 別のターミナルへはどう行くのですか？

Exercise 3 音声を聴いて、ダイアログの空所 1 ～ 4 を埋めましょう。次に 1 と 2 の質問に対して最も適切な答を a ～ c の中から選びましょう。

At the office Audio 1-30

Maya: Okay. ( ) ( ) ( ) ( ). Can I get you a tea or coffee?

うん、今日はこれでおしまい。紅茶かコーヒーはいかが？

Aoi: Sure. I'd like a cup of tea, please. No cream or sugar.

はい。紅茶をお願いします。ミルクとお砂糖は要りません。

Mr. Fong: ( ) ( ) ( ), how's the Osaka branch manager, Mr. Gordon doing?

ところで、大阪支社長のゴードンさんはお元気ですか？

Aoi: He's fine. You know, he's being transferred to the Honolulu branch next month.

元気にされています。えーっと、来月ホノルル支店に転勤される予定です。

Mr. Fong: Really? I bet he'll be happy with that since ( ) ( ) ( ).

本当ですか？彼はそこの出身だからその転勤はきっと大歓迎だろうね。

Aoi: Right. We think so, too.

その通りです。私たちもそう思っています。

Maya: Well, let's go and check in at the hotel. You'll be staying there for two nights.

さて、ホテルにチェックインしに行きましょう。二晩はホテルに滞在よ。

Aoi: Thank you.

ありがとうございます。

Mr. Fong: Will you be showing Aoi some apartments tomorrow?

明日いくつかアパートの物件をアオイに案内するのですか？

Maya: I sure will. I've already picked out 4( ) ( ) ( ) ( ) for her to see.

はい。すでに2〜3の物件をピックアップしています。

1. Which branch does Mr. Gordon work at?

a. The Honolulu branch   b. The Osaka branch   c. The Singapore branch

2. Where is he from?

a. US   b. Japan   c. Singapore

Restaurants by the Singapore River
along Boat Quay

Challenge Corner 1

● Audio 1-31

残りのダイアログを聴いて、1 ～ 3 の質問に対して最も適切な答を a ～ c の中から選びましょう。

In the hotel lobby

1. What time will Aoi and Maya meet again?

  a. At six thirty   b. At six forty-five   c. At seven

2. Where are they going to have the welcome party?

  a. At a restaurant   b. At the office   c. At the hotel

3. What are they most likely to eat at the welcome party?

  a. Steak   b. Pasta   c. Fish

Challenge Corner 2

ダイアログの音声を聴いて、　　の部分を書き取り、1 と 2 の質問に対して最も適切な答を a ～ c の中から選びましょう。

At the seafood restaurant   ● Audio 1-32

Mr. Fong: You joined our company about six months ago, didn't you?

Aoi: Yes, that's right.

Mr. Fong: Have you been to any other branches overseas?

1. When did Aoi start working for the company?

  a. In March   b. In April   c. In May

▶▶▶▶ ◀◀◀◀   ● Audio 1-33

Maya: Why don't we talk about tomorrow's schedule over breakfast?

Aoi: Sure. How about at the café   ?

Maya: Okay. Would eight o'clock be all right with you?

2. Where in the hotel is the café?

  a. On the first floor   b. On the second floor   c. On the third floor

Unit 5

First Posting

アパートを決める

マヤが引っ越しのお手伝いをしてくれるとのこと。アパートはマヤがピックアップしてくれていた素敵な物件の中の一つに即決。昼食後、アオイは当座の日用品を求めて近くのショッピングセンターへ。その後支社に戻り、支社に届いていたアオイの荷物を新しいアパートに配送してもらうよう手配。

 次の 1 ～ 8 の語または語句の最も適切な意味を下の a ～ h から選びましょう。
次に音声を聴いて単語の発音を確認しましょう。

• Audio 1-34

1. sleep like a log   **2.** sunny-side up   **3.** flat   **4.** landlady

5. charge an arm and a leg   **6.** move in   **7.** cozy   **8.** stuff

a. 引っ越す	b. 居心地が良い	c. 熟睡する	d. 物
e. 法外な金を請求する	f. アパート	g. 目玉焼き	h. 女性の大家

 次の 1 ～ 3 のダイアログの空所に入る最も適切なものを a ～ c の中から選びましょう。
次に質問の音声を聴いて、各ダイアログについての質問に答えましょう。

• Audio 1-35

At the café

1. Maya: Did you sleep well last night?

   Aoi: Yes, I did. ¹_____ a log. When I woke up, it was already seven o'clock.

   Maya: You must've been very tired yesterday.

   Answer

2. Waiter: How would you like your eggs?

   Maya: Scrambled, please. And I want some bacon, too.

   Aoi: ²_____ mine sunny-side up. And can I have a cup of coffee?

   Answer

3. Maya: Let's go check out some flats today. ³_____ a few for you.

   Aoi: Thanks very much for arranging to show me around.

   Maya: Oh, don't mention it. You helped me a lot when I was in Osaka.

   Answer

   a. I'd like to have   b. I slept like   c. I've picked out

　　1〜7の（　）内の語または語句を並べかえて英文を完成させましょう。ただし、文頭にくるものも小文字で与えています。次に音声を聴いて答を確認しましょう。

🔊 Audio 1-36

1. 将来は海外勤務をしたいと思っていました。
(work, in, I, to, future, abroad, wanted, the).

_____

2. 今回が初めての海外赴任になります。
(first, this, overseas, be, posting, my, will).

_____

3. シカゴ支店に転勤になりました。
(Chicago, been, to, the, I've, branch, transferred).

_____

4. 私の父は5年間エンジニアとして海外勤務をしました。
(five years, overseas, an, my father, spent, as, engineer).

_____

5. 今日、不動産業者と一緒にアパート探しをします。
Today (flat-hunting, with, I'm, agent, going, a real estate).

_____

6. 会社はすでに私のためにアパートを見つけていました。
(a, found, me, the company, flat, had, for) already.

_____

7. 同僚が私の引っ越しのお手伝いをしてくれました。
(my, helped, the, with, co-workers, me, moving).

_____

Exercise 2　　音声を聴いて、1〜5の空所を埋めましょう。次にa〜eの日本語の文の中から適切な意味をそれぞれ選び、英文の右の空欄に記入しましょう。

🔊 Audio 1-37

1. Is he likely to ^{1} _____ ^{2} _____ abroad?　　　　_____

2. Why do you want to ^{3} _____ ^{4} _____?　　　　_____

3. How often are you ^{5} _____ ^{6} ____ your company?　　　　_____

4. How long will your company be ^{7} _____ ^{8} _____ ^{9} _____?　　　　_____

5. Who will be ^{10} _____ ^{11} _____ an overseas branch next?　　　　_____

a. どれくらい頻繁に転勤になりますか？　　　b. どれくらいの期間貴社は海外に赴任させるんですか？
c. 彼は海外赴任の可能性はありますか？　　　d. 次は誰が海外に転勤になるのですか？
e. どうして海外勤務を希望するのですか？

Exercise 3 音声を聴いて、ダイアログの空所 1 ～ 4 を埋めましょう。次に 1 と 2 の質問に対して最も
適切な答を a ～ c の中から選びましょう。

In the apartment

●))) **Audio 1-38**

➤MRT=Mass Rapid Transit

Aoi: I've decided on this flat. There's (　　　) (　　　) (　　　) from the window and I can relax here.

このアパートに決めました。窓からの景色が良いし、リラックスできます。

Maya: I think you've made a good decision. It's in a good neighborhood, too.

ここに決めて良かったと思うわ。近所の環境が良いもの。

Aoi: Looks like it. It is very quiet and I feel at home.

そうみたいですね。とても静かだし、くつろげます。

Maya: It's (　　　) (　　　) (　　　). It is near an MRT station.

立地条件も良いのよ。MRT の駅も近くにあるわ。

Aoi: Now, that's important. I don't want to spend too much time commuting.

はい、それは大事です。通勤にそれほど時間をかけたくありませんから。

Maya: Right. I think it takes only twenty minutes from here to the office.

そうね。ここから支社まではわずか 20 分よ。

Aoi: Is it really that close? I can (　　　) (　　　) in the morning.

そんなに近いのですか?朝寝坊できます。

Maya: You know, there's a newly-built shopping center nearby.

えーっと、近くに新しくできたショッピングセンターがあるわ。

Aoi: Really? That's good. I need to buy some daily necessities and some groceries.

本当ですか?それはよかった。日常品や食料品を買わなくちゃいけないので。

Maya: All right. After we've talked (　　　) (　　　) (　　　), shall we go there?

そうね。大家さんとお話しした後、そこに行きましょうか?

1. How long does it take to get from the flat to the office?
　　a. Ten minutes　　　b. Thirty minutes　　　c. Twenty minutes

2. What are Aoi and Maya most likely to do next?
　　a. Buy some food　　　b. Talk with the landlady　　　c. Eat lunch

Challenge Corner 1

残りのダイアログを聴いて、1 ～ 3 の質問に対して最も適切な答を a ～ c の中から選びましょう。

At a café in the shopping center

1. What does Aoi need to buy?

   a. Soap   b. Shampoo   c. Both soap and shampoo

2. Where is the supermarket?

   a. On the first floor   b. On the second floor   c. On Basement 1

3. Who will pay for lunch?

   a. Aoi   b. Maya   c. It's not mentioned

Challenge Corner 2

ダイアログの音声を聴いて、 の部分を書き取り、1 と 2 の質問に対して最も適切な答を a ～ c の中から選びましょう。

At the office   Audio 1-40

Mr. Fong: Well, sounds like you found a good flat.

Aoi: I sure did. It's very cozy.   .

Mr. Fong: Have you got everything you need?

1. When will Aoi start living in the flat?

   a. Today   b. Tomorrow   c. The day after tomorrow

▶▶▶▶ ◀◀◀◀

Aoi: Do you know any moving companies?

Maya: Yes, but you won't need one.   . I can help you
         move all your things by car.

Aoi: But, there's a lot more stuff than I thought.

2. Is it expensive to use a moving company?

   a. Yes, it is.   b. No, it isn't.   c. It's not mentioned.

Unit 6

What a Cozy Place!

引っ越し作業

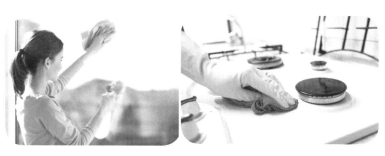

午前9時にホテルのロビーでマヤと合流してアオイのアパートへ。昨日会社から送ったアオイの荷物は午後1時頃届く予定なので、それまで部屋の掃除に専念。約束の時間よりも早く届いた荷物を整理した後、近くのホーカーズで夕食。さあ、明日からいよいよシンガポール支社での仕事が始まる。

次の1～8の語または語句の最も適切な意味を下のa～hから選びましょう。
次に音声を聴いて単語の発音を確認しましょう。

● **Audio 1-42**

1. around　　　　　**2.** wipe　　　　　**3.** bits and pieces　　　**4.** attractive

5. on the way to　　**6.** hawker center　**7.** reasonable　　　　　**8.** grab a bite

a. （…する）途中で　　　b. …頃　　　　c. …を拭く　　d. 魅力的な

e. （値段が）まあまあの　　f. 屋台を集めた屋外の施設　　g. 小物類　　h. 軽い食事をする

次の1～3のダイアログの空所に入る最も適切なものをa～cの中から選びましょう。
次に質問の音声を聴いて、各ダイアログについての質問に答えましょう。

● **Audio 1-43**

On the phone

1. **Maya:** Let's meet in the hotel lobby at around nine o'clock.

　　Aoi: Sure. ¹＿＿＿＿＿＿＿＿ to go out of your way, though.

　　Maya: I know, but I just want to help. That's all.

　　Answer

In the apartment

2. **Aoi:** ²＿＿＿＿＿＿＿＿ for coming here to help me today.

　　Maya: No problem. What time are you expecting the things you sent from the office?

　　Aoi: At about one o'clock, they said.

　　Answer

3. **Aoi:** Let's clean up in the morning.

　　Maya: Good idea! Why don't we do the kitchen first?

　　Aoi: OK. ³＿＿＿＿＿＿＿＿ to wipe the windows as well.

　　Answer

　　a. Thank you so much　　　b. We'll need　　　c. You don't need

26

1～7の（　）内の語または語句を並べかえて英文を完成させましょう。ただし、文頭にくるものも小文字で与えています。次に音声を聴いて答を確認しましょう。

Audio 1-44

1. いつ入居が可能ですか？

(possible, move, when, it, to, in, is)?

_____

2. 公共交通機関までどのくらいですか？

(public, is, how, it, transportation, far, to)?

_____

3. 駐車場代は家賃に含まれていません。

(rent, in, parking, the, not, is, included).

_____

4. 建物内に洗濯設備はあります。

(in, facilities, are, laundry, building, there, the).

_____

5. この建物ではゴミの分別をします。

(building, in, our, separate, this, we, trash).

_____

6. このアパートではタバコを吸ってはいけません。

(this flat, you, to, in, not, smoke, allowed, are).

_____

7. これはあなたへの引っ越し祝いです。

(present, a, this, for, housewarming, is, you).

_____

Exercise 2 音声を聴いて、1～5の空所を埋めましょう。次に a～e の日本語の文の中から適切な意味をそれぞれ選び、英文の右の空欄に記入しましょう。

Audio 1-45

1. ¹_____ ²_____ does the room face? _____

2. Is the flat ³_____ ⁴_____? _____

3. When is ⁵_____ ⁶_____ day? _____

4. ⁷_____ ⁸_____ are there in the kitchen? _____

5. Is there enough ⁹_____ ¹⁰_____ available? _____

a. ゴミの収集日はいつですか？   b. 台所にはどんな備品がありますか？

c. 収納スペースは十分にありますか？   d. 部屋の向きはどちらですか？

e. そのアパートは家具は全部そろっていますか？

Exercise 3   音声を聴いて、ダイアログの空所 1 ～ 4 を埋めましょう。次に 1 と 2 の質問に対して最も適切な答を a ～ c の中から選びましょう。

In the apartment   🔊 Audio 1-46

Maya: Can I (   ) (   ) (   ) your things?

荷物を取り出すのを手伝おうか？

Aoi: It's OK. I've almost finished. Oh, thanks for getting lunch.

大丈夫です。大体終わりましたから。あっ、昼食を買ってきてくれてありがとうございます。

Maya: Not at all. I was getting a little hungry myself anyway.

どういたしまして。ともかく私も少しお腹がすいてきていたし。

Aoi: We are lucky to have received my things from the delivery company

(   ) (   ) (   ).

約束の時間より早く運送会社から荷物が届けられてラッキーです。

Maya: We sure are. Now we have (   ) (   ) (   ) them.

そのとおり。さて、後はその荷物を整理するだけね。

Aoi: That's right. Let's start doing that after lunch.

そうですね。お昼を食べてから取りかかりましょう。

Maya: You can't work on an empty stomach, can you?

「腹が減っては戦はできぬ」よね。

Aoi: You can (   ) (   ) (   )!

その通りです。

Maya: Well, I've got some orange juice and milk.

えーっと、オレンジジュースと牛乳があるんだけど。

Aoi: Can I have some milk please?

牛乳をもらえますか？

1. Who bought lunch?
   a. Aoi   b. Maya   c. Both Aoi and Maya

2. What did Maya offer Aoi to drink?
   a. Orange juice   b. Milk   c. Both orange juice and milk

Challenge Corner 1

Challenge Corner ![1]

Challenge Corner 1

🔊 Audio 1-47

残りのダイアログを聴いて、1 〜 3 の質問に対して最も適切な答を a 〜 c の中から選びましょう。

1. Are most flats in Japan furnished?

    a. Yes, they are.   b. No, they aren't.   c. It's not mentioned.

2. Is Aoi's flat furnished?

    a. Yes, it is.   b. No, it isn't.   c. It's not mentioned.

3. Where did Aoi put the suitcases?

    a. In the kitchen   b. In the bedroom   c. In the closet

A luxury hawker style restaurant,
the Grand Hyatt hotel, Singapore

Newton Food Center, Singapore

Challenge Corner 2

ダイアログの音声を聴いて、　　の部分を書き取り、1 と 2 の質問に対して最も適切な答を a 〜 c の中から選びましょう。

▶▶▶▶ ◀◀◀◀   🔊 Audio 1-48

Aoi: I want to buy some bits and pieces for my flat.

Maya: in the neighborhood.

Aoi: Right. I think I saw some on the way to the shopping center yesterday.

Maya: Let's go and check them out.

1. What will Aoi and Maya be checking out?

    a. The neighborhood   b. Some attractive shops   c. The shopping center

▶▶▶▶ ◀◀◀◀   🔊 Audio 1-49

Maya: Why don't we drop by a hawker center for dinner?

Aoi: A hawker center? You mean a food court?

Maya: Yes. You can find a variety of dishes there and   .

Aoi: Sounds good. Let's grab a bite.

2. Is it expensive to eat at a hawker center?

    a. Yes, it is.   b. No, it isn't.   c. It's not mentioned.

引っ越し作業

Unit 7

First Day on the Job in Singapore

シンガポール支社勤務初日

今日から本格的にシンガポール支社での仕事が始まる。所属はマヤと同じ事業部。同僚に赴任の挨拶をした後、マヤが社内の主な部署を案内してくれる。希望していた海外赴任ではあったが内心少し不安だったので、同僚の笑顔に大いに救われる。午後、マヤが取引先企業について説明してくれた。

次の 1 ～ 8 の語または語句の最も適切な意味を下の a ～ h から選びましょう。
次に音声を聴いて単語の発音を確認しましょう。

● Audio 1-50

1. have butterflies in one's stomach **2.** belong to **3.** say hello to **4.** graduate school
5. accounting department **6.** general affairs **7.** How come? **8.** get audited

| a. …に所属する | b. 大学院 | c. …によろしくと言う | d. 胸がドキドキする |
| e. 経理部 | f. どうして | g. 会計監査を受ける | h. 総務 |

次の 1 ～ 3 のダイアログの空所に入る最も適切なものを a ～ c の中から選びましょう。
次に質問の音声を聴いて、各ダイアログについての質問に答えましょう。

● Audio 1-51

1. Aoi: Good morning, Maya.
   Maya: Good morning. You're in the office early.
   Aoi: Well, I got up at six because it's my first day. I guess ¹ _____.
   Answer

2. Maya: You belong to the same business section as me.
   Aoi: Right. Oh, boy. ² _____ in my stomach.
   Maya: Relax! We are all colleagues.
   Answer

3. Maya: It's nine o'clock. Let's go back to our section.
   Aoi: OK. Do you think I should say hello to everyone first?
   Maya: Sure. ³ _____.
   Answer

   a. I'll do the introductions   b. I'm a little nervous   c. I have butterflies

　1〜7の（　）内の語または語句を並べかえて英文を完成させましょう。ただし、文頭にくるものも小文字で与えています。次に音声を聴いて答を確認しましょう。

●))) Audio 1-52

1. 従業員の経歴は人事課で保管されています。
（ maintained, by, records, are, Human Resources, employee ）.

_____

2. 黄さんが当社の新しい受付係です。
（ at, Ms. Ko, new, company, receptionist, is, our, a ）.

_____

3. 役員会はひと月に一度会議があります。
（ a meeting, directors, has, a month, of, once, the board ）.

_____

4. かつて当社の本部はシドニーにありました。
（ in, our company's, be, Sydney, to, headquarters, used ）.

_____

5. ケンは旅行会社のマーケティング部門で働いています。
（ in, for, company, Ken, travel, marketing, works, a ）.

_____

6. 森山さんは他より安い価格を申し出ているようです。
（ offer, prices, seems, competitive, more, to, Ms. Moriyama ）.

_____

7. 今年度は黒字になりそうです。
（ being, the black, in, we, like, look ） this year.

_____

Exercise 2　音声を聴いて、1〜5の空所を埋めましょう。次にa〜eの日本語の文の中から適切な意味をそれぞれ選び、英文の右の空欄に記入しましょう。　●))) Audio 1-53

1. Where did you learn so much ^{1} _____ ^{2} _____ ?　　_____

2. Did you talk to the ^{3} _____ ^{4} _____ ?　　_____

3. Could I speak with the ^{5} _____ ^{6} _____ ?　　_____

4. ^{7} _____ ^{8} _____ is your R&D division on?　　_____

5. What is the ^{9} _____ ^{10} _____ for next year?　　_____

a. 工場長と話してもよろしいですか？　　b. 御社の研究開発部門は何階ですか？
c. どこで財務についてそれほど多く学んだのですか？　　d. 来年の経済の見通しはいかがですか？
e. 給与課に話しましたか？

Exercise 3 音声を聴いて、ダイアログの空所 1 ～ 4 を埋めましょう。次に 1 と 2 の質問に対して最も適切な答を a ～ c の中から選びましょう。

●)) **Audio 1-54**

Mr. Fong: Thank you for your wonderful self-introduction.
素敵な自己紹介でした。ありがとう。

Aoi: ( ) ( ) ( ).
恥ずかしい限りです。

Mr. Fong: No, 2( ) ( ) ( ). It was perfect. So when did you first come here?
いいえ、そんなことありません。とても良かったです。ところで、初めてここに来たのはいつのことですか？

Aoi: About a year and a half ago. I was in my third year at university.
1 年半ほど前のことです。大学の 3 年生でした。

Mr. Fong: Did you come here alone?
お一人で来られたのですか？

Aoi: No. I visited here with an 3( ) ( ) ( ) ( ) from Perth.
いいえ。パース出身のオーストラリア人の友人と一緒でした。

Mr. Fong: Oh, really? Did you go to Australia with your friend, too?
へー、そうですか。その友人とオーストラリアにも一緒に行ったのですか？

Aoi: Yes. I even stayed at her house. We also went to Sydney and Cairns.
はい。彼女の家にホームステイさえしました。シドニーとケアンズにも行きました。

Mr. Fong: Which city 4( ) ( ) ( ) ( )?
一番気に入ってるのはどの都市ですか？

Aoi: I liked Perth best.
パースです。

1. In what year of university did Aoi first visit Singapore?
   a. Second year   b. Third year   c. Fourth year

2. Which city in Australia is her favorite?
   a. Cairns   b. Sydney   c. Perth

Challenge Corner 1

残りのダイアログを聴いて、1～3の質問に対して最も適切な答をa～cの中から選びましょう。

1. How long did Aoi stay in Australia?
- a. Ten days
- b. Twelve days
- c. Fourteen days

2. How many cities in Australia did Aoi visit?
- a. One
- b. Two
- c. Three

3. What is Aoi's friend doing in Perth?
- a. Working
- b. Studying
- c. Graduating

Challenge Corner 2

ダイアログの音声を聴いて、＿＿の部分を書き取り、1と2の質問に対して最も適切な答をa～cの中から選びましょう。

Maya: These are conference rooms.

Aoi: How many are there?

Maya: There are six of them on this floor and ＿＿＿＿＿＿ .

Aoi: Wow! You must have many clients every day.

1. How many conference rooms are there altogether?
- Six
- Seven
- Eight

Maya: OK, The Accounting Department is here, and ＿＿＿＿＿＿ .

Aoi: How come everyone looks so busy?

Maya: I don't know. They may be getting audited soon.

Aoi: Audited? What does that mean? I don't understand.

2. Is the Accounting Department next to General Affairs?
- a. Yes, it is.
- b. No, it isn't.
- c. It's not mentioned.

Unit 8

Meeting a Business Client

商談に行く

アオイはマヤと共にスパイスを扱う会社に商談に行く。10時のアポに間に合うように支社を出て、MRTを利用して会社があるリトルインディアに向かう。商談後、支社に戻りフォング課長に商談の報告をする中、スパイスの会社のフー氏とフォング課長は高校時代からの友人だと聞かされて驚く。

次の1～8の語または語句の最も適切な意味を下のa～hから選びましょう。
次に音声を聴いて単語の発音を確認しましょう。

● Audio 1-58

1. dish   **2.** appointment   **3.** reception   **4.** reception room

5. unique   **6.** solve   **7.** sound like   **8.** each other

a. …を解決する	b. 料理	c. 約束	d. 応接室
e. 受付	f. 珍しい	g. お互いに	h. …のように聞こえる

次の1～3のダイアログの空所に入る最も適切なものをa～cの中から選びましょう。
次に質問の音声を聴いて、各ダイアログについての質問に答えましょう。

● Audio 1-59

At the office

1. Aoi: Good morning, Mr. Fong. Thank you for dinner last night.

    Mr. Fong: Good morning, Aoi. ¹_____.

    Aoi: I sure did. I loved every dish. It was so delicious.

    Answer

2. Maya: Would you like something to drink, Aoi?

    Aoi: No, thank you. ²_____ at a cafe.

    Maya: Are you sure? I make good coffee.

    Answer

3. Maya: Well, are you ready to go?

    Aoi: Sure. First to a spice company, right?

    Maya: That's right. ³_____ at ten.

    Answer

    a. I just had breakfast   b. We have an appointment   c. I hope you enjoyed it

Exercise 1　1〜7の（　）内の語または語句を並べかえて英文を完成させましょう。ただし、文頭にくるものも小文字で与えています。次に音声を聴いて答を確認しましょう。

● Audio 1-60

1. 紅梅商社の古谷ヒトシと申します。

(Kobai, am, Trading, from, I, Hitoshi Furutani).

_____

2. 10 時にフーさんとお会いする約束があります。

(have, Mr. Foo, at, I, appointment, an, with) ten.

_____

3. 海外部門で営業を担当しています。

(charge, am, sales, in, I, of, overseas).

_____

4. 今日はお越しいただきありがとうございます。

(for, you, very much, today, thank, coming).

_____

5. フーはまもなく参ります。

Mr. Foo (minute, here, be, in, will, a).

_____

6. 新製品をお見せしたいと思います。

(show, our, let, you, new products, me, please).

_____

7. 契約更新についてお話ししたいと思います。

(discuss, of, I'd, renewal, to, the contract, like).

_____

Exercise 2　音声を聴いて、1〜5の空所を埋めましょう。次に a 〜 e の日本語の文の中から適切な意味をそれぞれ選び、英文の右の空欄に記入しましょう。　● Audio 1-61

1. What kind of business are you [1] _____ [2] _____?　_____

2. Can I ask which company you [3] _____ [4] _____?　_____

3. Could you put on this [5] _____ [6] _____?　_____

4. Would ten o'clock be [7] _____ [8] _____ [9] _____?　_____

5. Could I [10] _____ [11] _____ in his department?　_____

a. 10 時はいかがでしょうか？　　　　　　b. どんな種類のお仕事をなさっているのですか？

c. 彼と同じ部署の方にお会いできますか？　　d. 会社名をお尋ねしてもよろしいでしょうか？

e. この来客証をおつけいただけますか？

Exercise 音声を聴いて、ダイアログの空所 1 ～ 4 を埋めましょう。次に 1 と 2 の質問に対して最も適切な答を a ～ c の中から選びましょう。

At reception   ● Audio 1-62

Maya: Hello, Susie. I'd like to see Mr. Foo of the Purchasing Division.

こんにちは、スージー。購買部のフーさんにお会いしたいのですが。

Receptionist: Do you have an appointment, Maya?

お約束はありますか、マヤ？

Maya: Yes. I have an appointment with him at ten o'clock.

ええ。10 時のお約束です。

Receptionist: Okay. I'll tell him that you're here.

わかりました。あなたが来社していることを彼に伝えます。

Maya: Thank you.

ありがとう。

Receptionist: Maya, Mr. Foo is (   ) (   ) (   ) at the moment. Would you mind waiting for a moment?

マヤ、今、フーは他のクライアントと打ち合わせ中です。少々お待ちいただけますか？

Maya: No, not at all. Oh, by the way, this is Aoi Manabe from our Osaka branch. She's been (   ) (   ) (   ) since April.

わかりました。あっ、ところで、こちらは弊社の大阪支社から転勤で来たマナベアオイです。

Aoi: How do you do? I'm Aoi. It's so good to meet you.

初めまして。アオイです。お会いできてとても嬉しいです。

Receptionist: How do you do, Aoi? Is this (   ) (   ) (   ) to Singapore?

初めましてアオイ。シンガポールは初めてですか？

Aoi: No. It's (   ) (   ) (   ). I first came here when I was a university student.

いいえ。今回で 2 度目です。大学生の時に来たことがあります。

---

1. What division does Mr. Foo belong to?
   a. Sales   b. Materials   c. Purchasing

2. What is Mr. Foo doing right now?
   a. Talking on the phone   b. Writing an email   c. Seeing another client

Challenge Corner 1

残りのダイアログを聴いて、1 ～ 3 の質問に対して最も適切な答を a ～ c の中から選びましょう。

In the reception room

1. How many people are there in the reception room?
  a. Two   b. Three   c. Four

2. Who's been waiting for Mr. Foo?
  a. Aoi   b. Maya   c. Both Aoi and Maya

3. When did Aoi come to Singapore?
  a. About four days ago   b. About ten days ago   c. About seven days ago

Challenge Corner 2

ダイアログの音声を聴いて、　の部分を書き取り、1 と 2 の質問に対して最も適切な答を a ～ c の中から選びましょう。

▶▶▶▶ ◀◀◀◀   Audio 1-64

Mr. Fong: What did you think of the spice company you visited this morning?

Aoi: It was very interesting. The company has a very unique feel about it.

Maya: Oh, Mr. Foo said   .

1. Who is going to Hong Kong on business?
  a. Aoi   b. Mr. Foo   c. Mr. Fong

▶▶▶▶ ◀◀◀◀   Audio 1-65

Mr. Fong: Mr. Foo is a friend from high school.

Aoi: Now, that solves it. It sounded like he knows a lot about you.

Mr. Fong: .

2. How long has Mr. Fong known Mr. Foo?
  a. 18 years   b. 20 years   c. 22 years

Unit 9

Making New Friends

友だちができる

アオイがシンガポール支社に赴任してから早ひと月半。アパート近くの公園でサンフランシスコ出身のカップル、クリスとドリーに出会う。アオイはサンフランシスコに滞在した経験があるので、話が盛り上がる。夫婦ともにアオイとちょうど同じ頃シンガポールに赴任して、半年ほど滞在する予定とのこと。

W 次の 1 〜 8 の語または語句の最も適切な意味を下の a 〜 h から選びましょう。
次に音声を聴いて単語の発音を確認しましょう。

● Audio 2-01

1. You know　　**2.** like　　**3.** yet　　**4.** posting

5. post　　**6.** place　　**7.** bring　　**8.** on the dot

a. まだ	b. ねえ	c. …のような	d. 時間通りに
e. ポスト・駐在	f. 家	g. …に転任させる	h. …を連れてくる

W 次の 1 〜 3 のダイアログの空所に入る最も適切なものを a 〜 c の中から選びましょう。
次に質問の音声を聴いて、各ダイアログについての質問に答えましょう。

In the park

● Audio 2-02

1. Aoi: Hi. Nice day, isn't it?
　Dolly: It sure is. You know, I've seen you here before. Do you live around here?
　Aoi: Yes, I do. I'm Aoi. From Japan. ¹_____ for a trading company here.
　Answer

2. Dolly: Oh, you're back, Chris… This is Aoi, from Japan. ²_____ on business.
　Chris: Hi, Aoi. Nice to meet you. I'm Chris. Dolly and I are from San Francisco.
　Aoi: Nice to meet you too, Chris.
　Answer

3. Dolly: ³_____ in October, and are staying till next March.
　Aoi: Are you here on business, too?
　Dolly: Yes. We work for an IT company.
　Answer

a. She's here　　b. I'm working　　c. We came here

Exercise 1　1～7の（　　）内の語または語句を並べかえて英文を完成させましょう。ただし、文頭にくるものも小文字で与えています。次に音声を聴いて答を確認しましょう。

🔊 Audio 2-03

1. なんて良い天気なんでしょう。
(it, a, day, what, is, beautiful)!

_____

2. 私の同僚を紹介したいのです。
(meet, my, I'd, you, to, colleague, like).

_____

3. 友だちを紹介させてください。
Please (introduce, friend, allow, my, to, me).

_____

4. ハインズさんに御社を紹介していただきました。
(referred, to, Mr. Hines, was, by, company, I, your).

_____

5. 上司からあなたのことは聞いておりました。
(heard, from, boss, about, I, you, my).

_____

6. 土曜日にお会いできるのを楽しみにしています。
(seeing, forward, I, on, you, to, look) Saturday.

_____

7. お父様によろしくお伝えください。
Please (to, father, my, regards, give, your, best).

_____

Exercise 2　音声を聴いて、1～5の空所を埋めましょう。次に a～e の日本語の文の中から適切な意味をそれぞれ選び、英文の右の空欄に記入しましょう。

🔊 Audio 2-04

1. Have [1]_____ [2]_____ met?　　　　　　_____

2. How do you [3]_____ [4]_____ [5]_____?　_____

3. Does it [6]_____ [7]_____ [8]_____ soon?　_____

4. What is the [9]_____ [10]_____ in the dish?　_____

5. Did you [11]_____ [12]_____ [13]_____ him?　_____

a. すぐにも雨が降りそうですか？　　　　b. その料理の隠し味は何ですか？

c. あなた方は以前お会いしたことはありますか？　　d. 彼にご挨拶しましたか？

e. あなた方はどうやってお知り合いになったのですか？

Exercise 　音声を聴いて、ダイアログの空所 1 ～ 4 を埋めましょう。次に 1 と 2 の質問に対して最も適切な答を a ～ c の中から選びましょう。

● Audio 2-05

Dolly: When did you come to Singapore?
シンガポールにはいつ来たのですか？

Aoi: I came here in October （　　　）（　　　）.
私も 10 月に来ました。

Dolly: Oh, （　　　）（　　　）（　　　）! Is this your first time working overseas?
あら、すごい偶然ですね！　今回が初めての海外赴任ですか？

Aoi: Yes, it is. How about you? Have you worked in （　　　）（　　　）（　　　）?
はい。お二人は？　どこか他の国で働いたことはありますか？

Dolly: Well, before coming here, we were in Japan.
ええ、ここに来る前は日本にいました。

Aoi: Where in Japan? Were you in Tokyo?
日本のどこですか？　東京でしたか？

Dolly: Yeah. We were there for six months. Then we transferred here.
ええ。そこに 6 か月いて、その後ここに転勤になりました。

Aoi: I see. You know, I've been to San Francisco once.
なるほど。あのう、私は一度サンフランシスコに行ったことがあるんです。

Dolly: Really? When did you go there?
本当？　いつ行きましたか？

Aoi: Five years ago when I was a （　　　）（　　　）（　　　）.
5 年前、大学一年生だった時です。

1. How many countries has Dolly been dispatched to up until now?
   a. One 　　　　　b. Two 　　　　　c. Three

2. How long did Dolly work in Japan?
   a. Four months 　　b. Six months 　　c. Eight months

Challenge Corner 1

Audio 2-06

残りのダイアログを聴いて、1 〜 3 の質問に対して最も適切な答を a 〜 c の中から選びましょう。

1. How long will Aoi be working in Singapore?

  a. One year   b. Two years   c. Three years

2. Will Chris be working in Singapore till next March?

  a. Yes, he will.   b. No, he won't.   c. It's not mentioned.

3. Where would Aoi like to be posted after Singapore?

  a. Tokyo   b. Sydney   c. It's not mentioned.

Challenge Corner 2

ダイアログの音声を聴いて、　　の部分を書き取り、1 と 2 の質問に対して最も適切な答を a 〜 c の中から選びましょう。

▶▶▶▶ ◀◀◀◀　Audio 2-07

Dolly: Do you have any plans for next weekend?

Aoi: I do on Friday night and Sunday, but not on Saturday.

Dolly: Good. _____. Would you like to come?

1. When is Dolly having a party at her house?

  a. Next Friday night   b. Next Saturday   c. Next Sunday

▶▶▶▶ ◀◀◀◀　Audio 2-08

Chris: You can bring a friend with you, if you want.

Aoi: Okay. I'll ask one of my Singaporean co-workers if she wants to come.

Chris: Good. _____.

2. What time will the party start?

  a. At five   b. At five-thirty   c. At six

Unit 10

Wining and Dining

接待のための準備

来週マレーシアのクアラルンプールから来社するお客様は火曜日から木曜日まで滞在予定。アオイとマヤはフォング課長から彼女の応対を任されたので、早速スケジュール作り。プレゼンの資料作り、ホテルやレストランの予約、支社の案内など……ビジネス拡大に向けて二人は頑張る。

 次の1～8の語または語句の最も適切な意味を下のa～hから選びましょう。次に音声を聴いて単語の発音を確認しましょう。

● Audio 2-09

1. employee　　**2.** detail　　**3.** look after　　**4.** gotcha

5. subject　　**6.** briefly　　**7.** impression　　**8.** contract

a. 了解	b. テーマ・項目	c. 従業員	d. …の世話をする
e. 詳細	f. 手短に	g. 印象	h. 契約

 次の1～3のダイアログの空所に入る最も適切なものをa～cの中から選びましょう。次に質問の音声を聴いて、各ダイアログについての質問に答えましょう。

At the office

● Audio 2-10

1.　Mr. Fong: Do you remember the spice company that Mr. Foo introduced to us?

　　Maya: You mean the one in Kuala Lumpur?

　　Mr. Fong: Yes. Two employees from the company want to ¹＿＿＿＿＿＿ next week.

　　Answer

2.　Maya: When next week are they coming?

　　Mr. Fong: I don't know the details yet, but I want you and Aoi to ²＿＿＿＿＿＿.

　　Maya: Sure. Let us know more as soon as you find out.

　　Answer

3.　Maya: You are not busy next week, are you, Aoi?

　　Aoi: No, I'm not. Why do you ask?

　　Maya: Well, you and I are supposed to ³＿＿＿＿＿＿ from Malaysia.

　　Answer

　　a. take care of the clients　　b. visit us　　c. look after them

Exercise 1   1〜7の（　　）内の語または語句を並べかえて英文を完成させましょう。ただし、文頭にくるものも小文字で与えています。次に音声を聴いて答を確認しましょう。

🔊 **Audio 2-11**

1. 特別なお客様を暖かく迎えてください。
Please (to, welcome, our, extend, a, special guest, warm).

_____

2. 私どもはそのお客様を接待する必要があります。
(and dine, the client, need, wine, to, we).

_____

3. 彼女が外国人のお客様の接待にあたっています。
(entertaining, foreign, is, charge, guests, she, of, in).

_____

4. 明日お客様をゴルフにお連れします。
(taking, to, clients, out, play, some, golf, I'm) tomorrow.

_____

5. ディナーにお連れしたいのですが。
(to, take, we, to, like, you, dinner, would).

_____

6. このレストランは一番おいしいステーキを出してくれます。
(serve, this restaurant, the, they, best, at, steak).

_____

7. 心温まるおもてなしをしていただき、誠にありがとうございました。
(for, the, very, reception, you, cordial, thank, much).

_____

Exercise 2   音声を聴いて、1〜5の空所を埋めましょう。次にa〜eの日本語の文の中から適切な意味をそれぞれ選び、英文の右の空欄に記入しましょう。

🔊 **Audio 2-12**

1. What do you ^{1} _____ ^{2} _____ eating?   _____

2. Would you like to ^{3} _____ ^{4} ____ for dinner?   _____

3. How about a drink ^{5} _____ ^{6} _____?   _____

4. Would you be ^{7} _____ ^{8} ____ going to a food fair?   _____

5. What time shall I ^{9} _____ ^{10} _____ ^{11} ____ from the hotel?   _____

a. 仕事後に一杯いかがですか？　　　　　b. 食のイベントに興味はおありですか？
c. 何時にホテルにお迎えに行きましょうか？　　d. 夕食をご一緒にいかがですか？
e. 何を召し上がりたい気分ですか？

音声を聴いて、ダイアログの空所 1 ~ 4 を埋めましょう。次に 1 と 2 の質問に対して最も適切な答を a ~ c の中から選びましょう。

● Audio 2-13

Mr. Fong: Mr. Foo said (　　　) (　　　) (　　　) would be coming next Tuesday.
フーさんによればその二人の社員は来週の火曜日に来るそうだよ。

Aoi: How long are they going to stay?
どれくらい滞在するのですか？

Mr. Fong: He said they'd be staying till Thursday.
木曜日までと彼は言ってたよ。

Aoi: Are we going to book a hotel for them?
彼女たちのホテルの予約は弊社でするのですか？

Mr. Fong: Yes. And will you (　　　) (　　　) (　　　) (　　　) on Wednesday night?
うん、そうして。で、水曜日の夕食の接待もお願いしていいかな？

Aoi: All right. I'll make a reservation.
わかりました。予約を入れておきます。

Mr. Fong: They don't have any dietary restrictions, so any food will be just fine.
彼女たちは食べられない物はないから、どんな食事でもまったく大丈夫だよ。

Aoi: OK, then. I'll make a reservation at the (　　　) (　　　) (　　　).
わかりました。じゃあ、いつものシーフードレストランを予約します。

Mr. Fong: I'll join you, so (　　　) (　　　) (　　　) when you book.
私も行くから、予約する際、人数に入れておいて。

Aoi: Sure. I'll let Maya know.
承知しました。マヤにも知らせておきます。

1. On which day will Aoi and Maya treat the clients to dinner?
   a. Tuesday　　　　b. Wednesday　　　　c. Both Tuesday and Wednesday

2. Who will make a reservation for dinner?
   a. Aoi　　　　b. Maya　　　　c. Mr. Fong

Challenge Corner

残りのダイアログを聴いて、1 ～ 3 の質問に対して最も適切な答を a ～ c の中から選びましょう。

1. Who will go to the airport to meet the clients?
   a. Aoi   b. Maya   c. Both Aoi and Maya

2. What time are the clients arriving at the airport?
   a. At two o'clock   b. At three o'clock   c. At four o'clock

3. What is the flight number?
   a. 245   b. 345   c. 254

Challenge Corner 2

ダイアログの音声を聴いて、　　の部分を書き取り、1 と 2 の質問に対して最も適切な答を a ～ c の中から選びましょう。

Audio 2-15

Maya: Before getting to the main subject,

Aoi: Can I help you prepare the materials for that?

Maya: Thank you. That'd be very helpful.

1. Who is going to introduce the company?
   a. Aoi   b. Maya   c. Neither of them

Audio 2-16

Mr. Fong: What time are you two leaving for the airport to meet them tomorrow?

Aoi: _____. It takes only thirty minutes to get there, so that'll give us enough time.

Mr. Fong: OK. We want to make a good impression on them and sign a contract later.

2. What time are Aoi and Maya leaving for the airport tomorrow?
   a. At 1:45 p.m.   b. At 2 p.m.   c. At 2:15 p.m.

Unit 11

Health Problems and Other Issues
体調をくずしたら

アオイがシンガポールに赴任して半年。最近ちょっと体調が悪かったので有給休暇をとってクリニックに行く。疲れがたまって風邪気味とのこと。支社長のピーターソンさんから少し休むようにと言われるがまま、2日休暇をとって休養。歯も痛み出したのでデンタルクリニックへ行き治療してもらう。

 次の1～8の語または語句の最も適切な意味を下のa～hから選びましょう。次に音声を聴いて単語の発音を確認しましょう。

● Audio 2-17

1. feverish **2.** medication **3.** symptom **4.** diarrhea

5. food poisoning **6.** sore throat **7.** stick one's tongue out **8.** in particular

| a. 特に | b. 熱のある | c. 喉の痛み | d. 薬 |
| e. 症状 | f. 舌を出す | g. 食中毒 | h. 下痢 |

次の1～3のダイアログの空所に入る最も適切なものをa～cの中から選びましょう。次に質問の音声を聴いて、各ダイアログについての質問に答えましょう。

On the phone ● Audio 2-18

1. Receptionist: Hello. Dr. Lim's office.
　　Aoi: 　　　Hello. ¹_____ to see Dr. Lim today?
　　Receptionist: Yes. You can see him at 11:30 a.m. May I have your name, please?
　　Answer

At Dr. Lim's office

2. Dr. Lim: ²_____ today?
　　Aoi: 　　　I'm feverish. And I have a stomachache. It started two days ago.
　　Dr. Lim: Are you currently taking any medications?
　　Answer

3. Dr. Lim: Do you have any other symptoms?
　　Aoi: 　　　I've had terrible diarrhea since yesterday.
　　Dr. Lim: You may have food poisoning. ³_____ the day before yesterday?
　　Answer

a. What did you eat　　b. Can I make an appointment　　c. What brings you here

Exercise 1　1〜7の（　　）内の語または語句を並べかえて英文を完成させましょう。ただし、文頭にくるものも小文字で与えています。次に音声を聴いて答を確認しましょう。

Audio 2-19

1. 名前が呼ばれるまで座ってお待ちください。
Please (seat, your, a, until, is, have, name, called).

_____

2. 確認のためにいくつか検査をする必要があります。
(run, to, need, tests, to, sure, some, make, I'll).

_____

3. 今日の会計は 150 ドルになります。
(consultation, $150, for, the bill, to, comes, today's).

_____

4. 歯茎に炎症を起こしていると思います。
(gums, think, infected, are, I, my).

_____

5. 痛みを感じたら右手を挙げてください。
(right hand, if, any, feel, raise, pain, you, your).

_____

6. ちょうど虫歯を治してもらったところです。
(have, cavity, just had, treated, I, a).

_____

7. 次回の予約を今お願いします。
(appointment, like, my, to, I, next, would, make) now.

_____

Exercise 2　音声を聴いて、1〜5の空所を埋めましょう。次に a 〜 e の日本語の文の中から適切な意味をそれぞれ選び、英文の右の空欄に記入しましょう。

Audio 2-20

1. ^{1} _____ ^{2} _____ can I see a doctor?　　　　_____

2. When did you notice ^{3} _____ ^{4} _____?　　　　_____

3. How long have you been ^{5} _____ ^{6} _____ ^{7} _____?　　　　_____

4. Is this treatment ^{8} _____ ^{9} _____ ^{10} _____?　　　　_____

5. Can I have a ^{11} _____ ^{12} _____?　　　　_____

a. 診断書をいただけますか？　　　　b. どれくらいこの状態が続いていますか？
c. すぐに診察してもらえますか？　　　d. いつごろこの症状に気づきましたか？
e. この治療に保険は適用されますか？

Exercise　音声を聴いて、ダイアログの空所 1 〜 4 を埋めましょう。次に 1 と 2 の質問に対して最も適切な答を a 〜 c の中から選びましょう。

At Dr. Huang's clinic　　　　　　　　　　• Audio 2-21

Receptionist: Hello. Can I help you?

こんにちは。いかがなさいましたか？

Aoi: Hello. I (　　　) (　　　) (　　　) a doctor.

こんにちは。診察していただきたいのですが。

Receptionist: Have you been to this clinic before?

以前このクリニックをご利用されたことはありますか？

Aoi: No, I haven't. It's (　　　) (　　　) (　　　).

いいえ。今回が初めてです。

Receptionist: All right, then I'll need you to (　　　) (　　　) (　　　) (　　　), please.

わかりました。それではこちらの用紙にご記入くださいますか。

Aoi: Sure... All done. Here you are.

はい……できました。どうぞ。

Receptionist: Thank you, Ms. Manabe. Do you have any insurance?

ありがとうございます、マナベ様。保険に入っていらっしゃいますか？

Aoi: Yes. I have an XYZ medical insurance policy. Can I use that?

はい。XYZ の医療保険に入っています。それを使えますか？

Receptionist: I think you can. Can I take a look at it, please?

使えると思います。見せていただけますか？

Aoi: Of course. (　　　) (　　　) (　　　).

もちろんです。さあ、どうぞ。

1. How many times has Aoi been to the clinic before?

　　Once　　　　　　　　Twice　　　　　　　Never

2. Can Aoi use her insurance at the clinic?

　　Yes, she can.　　　　　No, she can't.　　　　We don't know yet.

Challenge Corner 1

残りのダイアログを聴いて、1〜3の質問に対して最も適切な答を a〜c の中から選びましょう。

1. Does Aoi have a sore throat?

  a. Yes, she does.   b. No, she doesn't.   c. It's not mentioned.

2. When did she start feeling bad?

  a. On Monday   b. On Tuesday   c. On Wednesday

3. For how long has she been feeling bad?

  a. Two days   b. Three days   c. Four days

Challenge Corner 2

ダイアログの音声を聴いて、　　の部分を書き取り、1 と 2 の質問に対して最も適切な答を a〜c の中から選びましょう。

▶▶▶▶ ◀◀◀◀   Audio 2-23

Dentist: How can I help you today?

Aoi: _____, one of my fillings came out.

Dentist: All right. Please open your mouth and stick your tongue out.

1. When did Aoi's filling come out?

  a. Yesterday morning   b. Yesterday afternoon   c. Yesterday evening

▶▶▶▶ ◀◀◀◀   Audio 2-24

Aoi: My tooth hurts when I drink anything cold.

Dentist: Which one in particular hurts?

Aoi: _____ .

2. Which one of Aoi's teeth hurts? The...

  a. upper left back one   b. upper right back one   c. upper left back one

Unit 12

A Sales Presentation & Customer Complaints
プレゼン／クレーム処理

アオイは新規のお客様を訪問して会社紹介のプレゼンをする。お客様はシンガポールでも大手の食品会社。是非とも契約に結び付けたいので、今回は、このプレゼンのために準備した資料をマヤに目を通してもらい、万全の態勢で臨んだ。一方、マヤはクライアントからのクレーム処理に追われる。

次の 1 ～ 8 の語または語句の最も適切な意味を下の a ～ h から選びましょう。
次に音声を聴いて単語の発音を確認しましょう。

Audio 2-25

1. tip   **2.** handle   **3.** quantity   **4.** person in charge

5. invoice   **6.** agreement   **7.** grievance   **8.** instead of

a. 助言	b. 送り状	c. 担当者	d. …ではなくて
e. 数量	f. 苦情	g. 合意	h. …を処理する

次の 1 ～ 3 のダイアログの空所に入る最も適切なものを a ～ c の中から選びましょう。
次に質問の音声を聴いて、各ダイアログについての質問に答えましょう。

Audio 2-26

1.   **Aoi:**   Thank you so much for giving me some tips for the presentation.

     Maya: Don't mention it. We've got to enter into a contract with the company, after all.

     Aoi: I know. [1]_____ preparing the presentation materials.

     Answer

2.   **Maya:**   What time is your appointment with the company?

     Aoi: At 10:30, so [2]_____ in about fifteen minutes.

     Maya: I can give you a ride, since I'm going in the same direction to meet some clients.

     Answer

3.   **Maya:**   [3]_____ to handle a complaint today.

     Aoi: What is the complaint about?

     Maya: Remember we made a big mistake with the quantity of items on the invoice?

     Answer

   a. I have to meet this client   b. I spent a whole week   c. I'm leaving here

Exercise 1 　1～7の（　）内の語または語句を並べかえて英文を完成させましょう。ただし、文頭にくるものも小文字で与えています。次に音声を聴いて答を確認しましょう。

🔊 Audio 2-27

1. 私のプレゼンテーションのアウトラインはこちらです。

(presentation, is, outline, of, here, an, my).

_____

2. 私は 30 分ほどお話しさせていただく予定です。

(speaking, for, I'll, half, about, be, an hour).

_____

3. いつでも気軽にご質問してください。

Please (ask, free, feel, at, to, questions) any time.

_____

4. ご迷惑をおかけしてたいへん申し訳ございません。

(sorry, the, are, for, we, very, inconvenience).

_____

5. 教えていただきましてありがとうございます。

(the matter, to, you, for, our attention, thank, bringing).

_____

6. お支払いが遅れまして誠に申し訳ございません。

Please (payment, for, my apologies, in, accept, the delay).

_____

7. このようなことは二度と起こさないようにいたします。

(let, happen, won't, this, we, again).

_____

Exercise 2 　音声を聴いて、1～5の空所を埋めましょう。次に a～e の日本語の文の中から適切な意味をそれぞれ選び、英文の右の空欄に記入しましょう。

🔊 Audio 2-28

1. Does this ¹_____ ²_____ ³_____? 　　　　_____

2. Would you look at the ⁴_____ ⁵_____ ⁶_____? 　_____

3. How often do you get ⁷_____ ⁸_____ ⁹_____? 　_____

4. Would it be possible to ¹⁰_____ ¹¹____ ¹²_____? 　　_____

5. Could you tell me ¹³_____ ¹⁴____ ¹⁵____? 　　　　_____

a. どれくらい頻繁にお客様からクレームを受けるのですか？　　b. 返金は可能でしょうか？

c. ご質問の答えになりましたでしょうか？　　d. どうしたらいいか教えていただけますでしょうか？

e. 次の具体例をご覧いただけますでしょうか？

Exercise   音声を聴いて、ダイアログの空所 1 〜 4 を埋めましょう。次に 1 と 2 の質問に対して最も
適切な答を a 〜 c の中から選びましょう。

Sending SNS messages   Audio 2-29

Maya
Where are you now?

今どこ？

Aoi
I'm on the MRT, heading back to the office.

MRT で会社に戻っているところです。

Maya
When did you (   ) (   ) (   )?

いつプレゼンは終わったの？

Aoi
About half an hour ago.

30分ほど前です。

Maya
Would you like to catch up for lunch before going back to the office?

会社に戻る前にお昼を一緒にどう？

Aoi
Sure. Where can I meet you?

はい。どこに行けばいいですか？

Maya
How about at the Indian restaurant around the corner?

会社の近くにあるインド料理のレストランはどうかしら？

Aoi
Okay. It's ²(   ) (   ) (   )
(   ) now. I'll be there around twelve-thirty.

いいですね。今12時15分ですので、12時半頃にはそこに行けます。

Maya
Good. ³(   ) (   ) (   ).

良かった。バッチリね。

Aoi
All right. ⁴(   ) (   ) (   ) (   ).

はい。では、その時。

1. What time did Aoi finish her presentation?

a. About 11:30 a.m.   b. About 11:45 a.m.   c. About noon

2. What are Aoi and Maya most likely to do next?

a. Go back to the office   b. Have lunch together   c. See their customers

52

Challenge Corner 1

Audio 2-30

残りのダイアログを聴いて、1 ～ 3 の質問に対して最も適切な答を a ～ c の中から選びましょう。

1. Who made the presentation?

   a. Aoi　　　　　　　b. Maya　　　　　　c. Both Aoi and Maya

2. When is Aoi going to see the client next?

   a. Today　　　　　　b. Tomorrow　　　　c. In a week

3. How many people from the client company are coming to Aoi's office?

   a. Only one　　　　　b. Two　　　　　　c. More than two

Challenge Corner 2

ダイアログの音声を聴いて、　の部分を書き取り、1 と 2 の質問に対して最も適切な答を a ～ c の中から選びましょう。

▶▶▶▶ ◀◀◀◀　　　　　　　　Audio 2-31

Aoi: Well, how did your handling of that customer complaint go today?

Maya: They were pretty upset at first, but we eventually reached an agreement.

Aoi: Good! ＿＿＿＿＿＿＿＿＿＿ at handling client grievances.

1. Is Aoi better than Maya at handling customer complaints?

   a. Yes, she is.　　　b. No, she isn't.　　　c. We don't know.

▶▶▶▶ ◀◀◀◀　　　　　　　　Audio 2-32

Aoi: What was wrong with the invoice?

Maya: ＿＿＿＿＿＿＿＿＿＿. It should have been $30,000, instead of $40,000.

Aoi: How could we have made such a careless mistake!

2. How much should they have charged on the invoice?

   a. $30,000　　　　b. $40,000　　　　c. $70,000

プレゼン／クレーム処理

Unit 13

Catching up with an Old Friend in Perth

有給休暇をとってパースへ

アオイは２日間有給休暇をとって友人のエミリーに会いにパースへ。エミリーは博士課程を修了して博士論文もほとんど書き終わり、西オーストラリア大学で教員公募に応募したいと考えている。もし公募がなければ、アオイの母校へ行って教育・研究に携わりたいらしい。二人の久しぶりの再会。

次の１～８の語または語句の最も適切な意味を下のa～hから選びましょう。
次に音声を聴いて単語の発音を確認しましょう。　● Audio 2-33

1. Long time no see.　**2.** experienced　**3.** muggy　**4.** look for

5. doctoral dissertation　**6.** competitive　**7.** venture　**8.** actually

a. 経験を積んだ	b. 蒸し暑い	c. 久しぶり	d. （人が）危険を冒して立ち向かう
e. 競争の激しい	f. 博士論文	g. 実は	h. …を探す

次の１～３のダイアログの空所に入る最も適切なものをa～cの中から選びましょう。
次に質問の音声を聴いて、各ダイアログについての質問に答えましょう。

In the arrivals lounge　● Audio 2-34

1.　Emily: Long time no see.

　　Aoi:　You're not wrong. It must be over a year since I last saw you in Japan.

　　Emily: ¹ _____ an experienced businessperson.

　　Answer

2.　Emily: What is it like to live in Singapore?

　　Aoi:　Well, it's very hot and muggy, but I love it.

　　Emily: Good. ² _____ everything's been going so well for you.

　　Answer

3.　Aoi:　How are your parents?

　　Emily: They're fine. I still live with them. My dad is in Sydney on business now.

　　Aoi:　Really? That's too bad. ³ _____ work with him.

　　Answer

　　a. It sounds like　　b. I wanted to talk about　　c. You already look like

54

　1〜7の（　　）内の語または語句を並べかえて英文を完成させましょう。ただし、文頭にくるものも小文字で与えています。次に音声を聴いて答を確認しましょう。

● Audio 2-35

1. 従業員は一年で 2 週間の年次休暇がもらえます。

　（ receive, leave, employees, two weeks', annual).

_____

2. 日本では長期にわたる休暇を取るのは難しいです

　（ a, it, vacation, take, difficult, is, to, long) in Japan.

_____

3. 私の友人は今年の有給休暇がまだ 10 日残っています。

　（ has, paid days off, still, ten, my friend, more) this year.

_____

4. 彼女は産休をとるようになっています。

　（ going to, maternity, she, be taking, leave, is).

_____

5. 彼は 6 月から育児休暇中です。

　（ on, since, he's, leave, June, parental, been).

_____

6. 彼女は去年の夏休暇でハワイ旅行に行きました。

　（ to, on, Hawaii, went, summer, vacation, she, last).

_____

7. あなたとご家族にとって良い休暇になりますように。

　（ a, you, holiday, wish, happy, your family, I, and ）

_____

Exercise 2　音声を聴いて、1〜5 の空所を埋めましょう。次に a〜e の日本語の文の中から適切な意味をそれぞれ選び、英文の右の空欄に記入しましょう。

● Audio 2-36

1. Could I take ____ ¹ _____ ² _____ ³ next Thursday?　_____

2. How many days ____ ⁴ _____ ⁵ _____ ⁶ do you get?　_____

3. Have you _____ ⁷ ____ ⁸ all of your paid holidays?　_____

4. Do you have any plans for the _____ ⁹-_____ ¹⁰ _____ ¹¹ ?　_____

5. Can I ¹² _____ ¹³ _____ my paid holidays to the following year?　_____

a. 有給休暇を翌年に持ち越すことができますか？　　b. 5 連休の予定は何かありますか？

c. 有給休暇は使い切りましたか？　　d. 年次有給休暇は何日ありますか？

e. 来週の木曜日に休みをもらえますか？

Exercise 3 音声を聴いて、ダイアログの空所 1 ～ 4 を埋めましょう。次に 1 と 2 の質問に対して最も適切な答を a ～ c の中から選びましょう。

• Audio 2-37

➤UWA=The University of Western Australia

Aoi: So, what have you been up to?

ところで、最近はどうしてる？

Emily: Well, I finished my doctoral program, and…

えっと、博士課程は終わって……

Aoi: Have you ( ) ( ) ( ) ( )?

論文は書き終わったの？

Emily: You mean the doctoral dissertation?

博士論文のこと？

Aoi: Yes. That's it. Have you?

ええ。それそれ。終わった？

Emily: Almost. I'll probably finish writing it ( ) ( ) ( ) ( ).

ほとんどね。おそらく1週間後には完成よ。

Aoi: Good for you, Emily! Now you'll have to look for a job.

やったわね、エミリー！　今度は仕事を探さないとね。

Emily: That's right. I want to get a job as a university lecturer here in Perth.

その通り。ここパースで大学教員の職に就きたいと思っているわ。

Aoi: Are there any openings for ( ) ( ) ( ) ( ) here?

どこかの大学で教員の公募をしてるの？

Emily: Yes. UWA is looking for a full-time lecturer with my background.

うん。西オーストラリア大学が私のような経歴を持つ常勤の講師を募集しているの。

Aoi: ( ) ( )!

幸運を祈ってるわ！

1. When will Emily probably finish writing her doctoral dissertation?
   a. In a day or two　　b. In three or four days　　c. In seven or eight days

2. Where does Emily want to work?
   a. In Osaka　　　　b. In Perth　　　　c. In neither Osaka nor Perth

Challenge Corner 1

🔊 Audio 2-38

残りのダイアログを聴いて、1 ～ 3 の質問に対して最も適切な答を a ～ c の中から選びましょう。

1. Has Emily applied for the teaching position at Aoi's university?

    a. Yes, she has.   b. No, she hasn't.   c. We don't know.

2. Is it easy to get a teaching position at UWA?

    a. Yes, it is   b. No, it isn't.   c. We can't tell.

3. What will Aoi tell her professor about?

    a. Herself   b. Her university   c. Emily

Challenge Corner 2

ダイアログの音声を聴いて、　の部分を書き取り、1 と 2 の質問に対して最も適切な答を a ～ c の中から選びましょう。

▶▶▶▶ ◀◀◀◀   🔊 Audio 2-39

Mrs. Atkins: It's very good to see you again, Aoi. You look wonderful.

Aoi: Thank you. I'm so glad to see you, too. Too bad I can't see Mr. Atkins.

Mrs. Atkins: Actually, he has had a change of plans, and

.

1. When on Saturday is Mr. Atkins coming home?

    a. At about 2 p.m.   b. At about 5 p.m.   c. At midnight

▶▶▶▶ ◀◀◀◀   🔊 Audio 2-40

Mrs. Atkins: Does your company have any branches in Australia?

Aoi: .

Mrs. Atkins: Oh, so you may be working in Australia one day.

2. How many branches does Aoi's company have in Australia?

    a. One   b. Two   c. Three

A Business Trip to Indonesia and Hong Kong

出張―インドネシア／香港

アオイはインターナショナル・フードフェアを視察するため、来週は香港出張。一方、マヤはジャワ島の西ジャワ州にあるタシクマラヤへ出張。ここではめずらしいアラビカ種のコーヒーを栽培するコーヒー園がある。マヤはそのコーヒー園と近隣にある他のコーヒー園の視察にやって来たのだ。

次の 1 ～ 8 の語または語句の最も適切な意味を下の a ～ h から選びましょう。
次に音声を聴いて単語の発音を確認しましょう。

● Audio 2-41

1. food fair   **2.** get in touch with   **3.** else   **4.** twice

5. close to   **6.** freshly-ground   **7.** aroma   **8.** reckon

a. 二度	b. …だと考える	c. 挽きたての	d. 食のイベント
e. …に近い	f. 他に	g. かおり	h. …と連絡を取る

次の 1 ～ 3 のダイアログの空所に入る最も適切なものを a ～ c の中から選びましょう。
次に質問の音声を聴いて、各ダイアログについての質問に答えましょう。

At the office

● Audio 2-42

1. Mr. Fong: I want you to go to a food fair in Bangkok next week.
   Aoi: To the Bangkok International Food Fair you were talking about?
   Mr. Fong: Yes. I want you to go there and ¹_____.
   Answer

2. Mr, Fong: I heard one employee from the Hong Kong branch will be there, too.
   Aoi: Really? That's good to know. I wonder who it'll be.
   Mr. Fong: Well, why don't you ²_____ to find out?
   Answer

3. Mr. Fong: Have you decided when you're going to the food fair in Bangkok?
   Aoi: Yes. I'll be leaving here next Tuesday and coming back on Thursday.
   Mr. Fong: The General Affairs Section will help you ³_____.
   Answer

   a. get in touch with them   b. make airline and hotel reservations
   c. look for new clients

1〜7の（　　）内の語または語句を並べかえて英文を完成させましょう。ただし、文頭に くるものも小文字で与えています。次に音声を聴いて答を確認しましょう。

● **Audio 2-43**

1. 彼女は海外出張中です。

(overseas, trip, she, on, business, is, an).

_____

2. 私は出張から戻ってきたばかりです。

(just returned, a, have, business, from, I, trip).

_____

3. 経費はあとで清算します。

(your, will, for, reimbursed, you, expenses, be) later.

_____

4. 遠くからお越しいただいてありがとうございます。

(for, thank, all, coming, way, you, the) here.

_____

5. 実際の生産ラインを見せていただけますとありがたいのですが。

(see, actual, to, line, we'd, the, production, like).

_____

6. 御礼の言葉もございません。

(you, don't, how, I, enough, thank, to, know).

_____

7. 私は返礼できる機会を楽しみにしています。

(forward, the, look, to, reciprocate, to, I, opportunity).

_____

Exercise 2 音声を聴いて、1〜5の空所を埋めましょう。次に a 〜 e の日本語の文の中から適切な意 味をそれぞれ選び、英文の右の空欄に記入しましょう。 ● **Audio 2-44**

1. Do you go on a business trip ¹_____ ²___ ³_____?　　　　　_____

2. Did you ⁴_____ ⁵____ ⁶_____ with the client?　　　　_____

3. How long are you going to ⁷____ ⁸_____?　　　　_____

4. Could you ⁹_____ ¹⁰___ ¹¹_____ for Mr. Kite?　　　　_____

5. Why don't you ¹²_____ ¹³_____ ¹⁴_____ us to the party?　　　　_____

a. 取引先との面会の約束は取れましたか？　　　b. パーティにご一緒しませんか？

c. カイトさんに伝言をお願いできますでしょうか？　　　d. 月に一度は出張に行きますか？

e. 不在にする期間はどれくらいですか？

Exercise 3　音声を聴いて、ダイアログの空所 1 〜 4 を埋めましょう。次に 1 と 2 の質問に対して最も適切な答を a 〜 c の中から選びましょう。

🔊 Audio 2-45

Aoi: Hi, Maya. When did you get back from Indonesia?

マヤ、こんにちは。インドネシアからいつ帰ってきたのですか？

Maya: Oh, hi Aoi. I came back ¹(　　　)(　　　)(　　　)(　　　).

あ、アオイ、こんにちは。先週の金曜日の夜遅くよ。

Aoi: Well, how were the coffee farms in Tasikmalaya?

ところで、タシクマラヤのコーヒー園はどうでしたか？

Maya: Wonderful! They produce rare Arabica coffee, and it tastes so good.

すばらしい！　めずらしいアラビカ種のコーヒーを作っていて、とてもおいしかった。

Aoi: Did you ²(　　　)(　　　)(　　　)(　　　)?

その豆を持ちかえってきました？

Maya: Sure. I'll make you some coffee later. So, ³(　　　)(　　　)(　　　)(　　　)?

もちろんよ。後で煎れるわね。ところで、あなたはどう？

Aoi: I'm going to Bangkok tomorrow for three days.

明日から 3 日間バンコクに行きます。

Maya: Really? What for?

本当？　どうして？

Aoi: Remember the international food fair Mr. Fong was talking about?

フォングさんが話してたインターナショナル・フードフェアを覚えていますか？

Maya: Yeah… are you going there?

ええ……そこに行くの？

Aoi: I certainly am. I'm really ⁴(　　　)(　　　)(　　　)(　　　).

はい。そのフェアの視察を楽しみにしています。

---

1. What time did Maya most likely come back from Indonesia last Friday?

　　a. Around 5 p.m.　　b. Around 7:30 p.m.　　c. Around 10 p.m.

2. How many days will Aoi be staying in Bangkok?

　　a. Two days　　b. Three days　　c. Four days

Challenge Corner 1

Audio 2-46

残りのダイアログを聴いて、1 ～ 3 の質問に対して最も適切な答を a ～ c の中から選びましょう。

1. Has Aoi been to Bangkok before?

　a. Yes, she has.　　　b. No, she hasn't.　　　c. We don't know.

2. How many times has Maya been to Thailand?

　a. Once　　　b. Twice　　　c. Three times

3. Does Aoi know where Pattaya is?

　a. Yes, she does.　　　b. No, she doesn't.　　　c. We can't tell.

Kopi Sidikalang (Sidikalang Coffee Bean), Tasikmalaya

Challenge Corner 2

ダイアログの音声を聴いて、　の部分を書き取り、1 と 2 の質問に対して最も適切な答を a ～ c の中から選びましょう。

▶▶▶▶ ◀◀◀◀
Audio 2-47

Maya: So, what do you think about the coffee from Tasikmalaya?

Aoi: ＿＿＿＿＿＿＿＿＿＿＿ of the freshly-ground beans.

Maya: I'm glad you do. I reckon it will sell well.

1. Has Aoi tried the coffee from Tasikmalaya?

　a. Yes, she has.　　　b. No, she hasn't.　　　c. We can't tell.

▶▶▶▶ ◀◀◀◀
Audio 2-48

Aoi: I'm thinking of taking a paid vacation sometime next month.

Maya: Oh, really? Are you going back to Kansai to meet your friends?

Aoi: ＿＿＿＿＿＿＿＿＿＿＿ to see an Australian friend of mine.

2. Where is Aoi most likely to go during her vacation next month?

　a. Kansai　　　b. Perth　　　c. Both Kansai and Perth

出張―インドネシア―香港

Unit 15

A New Assignment

海外転勤の内示 2

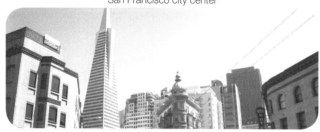

San Francisco city center

シンガポールに赴任して 1 年が経過したアオイにサンフランシスコ支社への転勤命令が下る。シドニー支社への転勤を希望していたのでこの転勤は寝耳に水。でも、サンフランシスコには母の友人のペギーさんやその娘ジュディもいるので結構楽しみ。一方、マヤは香港支社への転勤を告げられる。

次の 1 〜 8 の語または語句の最も適切な意味を下の a 〜 h から選びましょう。
次に音声を聴いて単語の発音を確認しましょう。

• **Audio 2-49**

1. You know something?　　**2.** blame　　**3.** miss　　**4.** dim sum

5. You can say that again.　　**6.** look forward to　　**7.** commute　　**8.** get married

a. 点心（中国料理）	b. …を楽しみに待つ	c. 通勤する	d. 結婚する
e. …を責める	f. …をなつかしく思う	g. ねえ、聞いて	h. 全くその通り

次の 1 〜 3 のダイアログの空所に入る最も適切なものを a 〜 c の中から選びましょう。
次に質問の音声を聴いて、各ダイアログについての質問に答えましょう。

• **Audio 2-50**

1. Maya: Aoi, where have you been? Mr. Peterson has been looking for you.
　Aoi: I was in the Accounting Department on the third floor. Where did he go?
　Maya: I think ¹ _____ to his office.
　Answer

2. Aoi: Good morning Mr. Peterson. What is it you want to see me about?
　Mr. Peterson: Well, ² _____ to the San Francisco branch.
　Aoi: Really? What a surprise! I thought I'd be transferred to Sydney.
　Answer

3. Maya: So, when are you moving to San Francisco?
　Aoi: I haven't decided yet, but it'll be around the end of this month.
　Maya: You know something? ³ _____, too.
　Answer

　a. we've decided to transfer you　　　b. I may be transferred
　c. he has gone back

Exercise 1　1～7の（　）内の語または語句を並べかえて英文を完成させましょう。ただし、文頭にくるものも小文字で与えています。次に音声を聴いて答を確認しましょう。

● Audio 2-51

1. 人事異動は 4 月に行われます。
(personnel, a, in, is, reshuffle, there, April).

_____

2. 社内の組織変更がありました。
(change, we, an, organization, had, internal, of).

_____

3. 新しい支社長は大阪より赴任します。
(new, transferring, our, from, branch manager, will be, Osaka).

_____

4. 私の人事異動のお知らせでメールいたしております。
(writing, my, I, you, to, am, about, transfer).

_____

5. 上司と希望の部署について話をしました。
(my boss, division, about, I, my, with, preferred, talked).

_____

6. 明日は人事異動の発表があります。
(employee, is, of, movements, tomorrow, for, the day, the announcement).

_____

7. 彼女は一身上の理由で退社します。
(for, going, resign, reasons, she, personal, is, to).

_____

Exercise 2　音声を聴いて、1～5 の空所を埋めましょう。次に a～e の日本語の文の中から適切な意味をそれぞれ選び、英文の右の空欄に記入しましょう。

● Audio 2-52

1. Who is the new ¹_____ ²_____ ³_____?　　_____

2. Can you attend the ⁴_____ ⁵_____?　　_____

3. How long is it since you were ⁶_____ ⁷_____ ⁸_____?　　_____

4. ⁹_____ ¹⁰_____ has he moved to?　　_____

5. When do you start working in the ¹¹_____ ¹²_____?　　_____

a. シドニーに赴任してどれくらい経ちますか？　　b. 彼はどの部署に異動しましたか？

c. 営業部での仕事はいつからですか？　　d. 送別会には参加できますか？

e. 貴社の新しい CEO はどなたですか？

Exercise 3 音声を聴いて、電子メールの空所 1 〜 4 を埋めましょう。次に 1 と 2 の質問に対して最も適切な答を a 〜 c の中から選びましょう。

🔊 **Audio 2-53**

Dear Judy,

It's been ages since I ( ) ( ) ( ) ( ) you last. How are you and your family? I hope you are well. My family back in Japan has been doing OK.

I told you that I was working for a foreign trading company in Singapore. Well, it was just yesterday that I was told that I'd be transferred to the San Francisco branch. I'm going there ( ) ( ) ( ) ( ). I'll probably start work on the first day of May.

My mother is a little ( ) ( ) ( ). She told me that she'd be coming to see me every ( ) ( ) ( ) ( ). She must miss San Francisco a lot. I don't blame her for that. I feel very lucky to be transferred there myself.

1. When is Aoi going to San Francisco?
   a. Around April 9th   b. Around April 15th   c. Around April 27th

2. When will Aoi start work in San Francisco?
   a. May 10th   b. May 5th   c. May 1st

San Francisco's Chinatown

Chinese restaurant in San Francisco

Challenge Corner 1

残りの電子メールを読んで、1 ～ 3 の質問に対して最も適切な答を a ～ c の中から選びましょう。

My office is in the Financial District, which is close to Chinatown. You know how much I like dim sum. Who knows? I may go there to have dim sum for lunch every day.

I'm wondering whether I should live in the city, in Oakland, or in Berkeley. I'm going to get an international driver's license, but I don't want to commute by car. Can you give me some advice about where to live?

I'm looking forward to seeing you in San Francisco very soon.

Your friend,
Aoi

1. Is Chinatown close to where Aoi will be working?
   a. Yes, it is.   b. No, it isn't.   c. It is not mentioned.

2. What kind of driver's license will she get?
   a. A Japanese one   b. An American one   c. An international one

3. Is she thinking of driving to work?
   a. Yes, she is.   b. No, she isn't.   c. Yes, she has a car.

Challenge Corner 2

ダイアログの音声を聴いて、　　の部分を書き取り、1 と 2 の質問に対して最も適切な答を a ～ c の中から選びましょう。

▶▶▶▶ ◀◀◀◀

Maya: I have some big news to tell you, too.

Aoi: Oh, what is it?   ?

Maya: Wrong! I've been asked to move to the Hong Kong branch.

1. Is Maya going to get married soon?

   a. Yes, she is.   b. No, she isn't.   c. It is not mentioned.

▶▶▶▶ ◀◀◀◀

Aoi: I'll be working in San Francisco, and you'll be in Hong Kong.

Maya: I guess transferring is just part of the job of a businessperson.

Aoi: You can say that again. Who knows?

.

2. Who will be working in Hong Kong?
   a. Aoi   b. Maya   c. Both Aoi and Maya

海外転勤の内示 2

First Time Working Abroad
はじめての英会話コミュニケーション：就職編

2020 年 4 月 10 日　初版第 1 刷発行
2023 年 3 月 10 日　初版第 2 刷発行

著　者　行時 潔／今川京子／Antony J. Parker

発行者　森　信久
発行所　**株式会社　松柏社**
　　　　〒 102-0072　東京都千代田区飯田橋 1-6-1
　　　　TEL　03 (3230) 4813（代表）
　　　　FAX　03 (3230) 4857
　　　　http://www.shohakusha.com
　　　　e-mail: info@shohakusha.com

装丁　　小島トシノブ（NONdesign）
挿絵　　うえむらのぶこ

印刷・製本　日経印刷株式会社

略号＝ 755
ISBN978-4-88198-755-1
Copyright © 2020 by Kiyoshi Yukitoki, Kyoko Imagawa & Antony J. Parker